3/98

17.95

Ⅱ0622920

A M E R I C A N
P R O F I L E S

Twentieth-Century
Writers
1950–1990

■

Tom Verde

Facts On File, Inc.

This one's for Kate

Twentieth-Century Writers 1950–1990

Facts On File, Inc.
11 Penn Plaza
New York, NY 10001

Library of Congress Cataloging-in-Publication Data

Verde, Thomas A. (Thomas Aquinas), 1958–
   Twentieth-century writers, 1950–1990 / Tom Verde.
     p.   cm. — (American profiles)
   Includes bibliographical references (p.) and index.
   Summary: This collection of short literary biographies of American writers of the second half of the twentieth century is the continuation of Twentieth-century Writers 1900–1950.
   ISBN 0-8160-2967-9 (alk. paper)
   1. Authors, American—20th century—Biography—Juvenile literature.   [1. Authors, American.]   I. Title.   II. Series: American profiles (Facts On File, Inc.)
PS129.V48   1996
810.9'0054—dc20
[B]   95-35341

Facts On File books are available at special discounts when purchased in bulk quantities for businesses, associations, institutions, or sales promotions. Please call our Special Sales Department in New York at 212/967-8800 or 800/322-8755.

Cover design by Matt Galemmo

This book is printed on acid-free paper

Printed in the United States of America

MP FOF 10 9 8 7 6 5 4 3 2

ACKNOWLEDGMENTS

Deep appreciation goes to my friend and colleague James Warren for his unending patience, understanding, and readiness to go to bat for me; to my editor Michelle Fellner, for her gentle yet persistent impatience and without whose regular phone calls and finagling this project might never have been completed; and of course to my loving and supportive wife, Kate Robins, my best editor and best friend.

Thanks also go to the following institutions for providing illustrations: the National Archives, the Library of Congress, Georgia College, Valley Forge Military Academy and College, General Electric Co., and the Mississippi Department of Archives and History.

Contents

Introduction

*T*he period of American literary history covered in this book commenced in an era characterized by both calm and fear. The United States had emerged as a world power in the wake of World War II; returning GIs looked forward to realizing the American dream under a better economy; and the sanctity and security of the American family remained intact, despite the fears of some parents that civilization was threatened by a hip-twitching, lip-curling rock-and-roller from Tupelo, Mississippi, named Elvis Aaron Presley.

But there were real threats brewing, both at home and abroad. Russia, once an ally, had become a powerful foe as the globe became divided between the Communist bloc and the free world. The Cold War and the threat of nuclear destruction were genuine fears, underscored by Soviet leader Nikita Khrushchev's promise to "bury" the United States as a political power. It was a time of fallout shelters in the home and children practicing "duck and cover" maneuvers in the classroom, in anticipation of nuclear attack.

In the streets of America, citizens marched, and later rioted, in protest against the Vietnam War, in favor of civil rights, against civil rights, for equal rights for women. The assasination of President John F. Kennedy stunned the nation, giving way, it seemed, to a politically charged culture of violence in which more leaders fell—Malcom X, Martin Luther King, Robert Kennedy—and institutions, such as Kent State University or the 1968 Democratic National Convention, became scenes of bloody havoc. The country's moral fabric appeared to be unraveling as children no longer obeyed their parents, illegal drug use escalated among the middle class, and permissiveness saturated every aspect of culture from dating to art, fashion, and music. By the time of the Watergate scandal, Americans had lost faith in their political leaders as well.

Introduction

These events left us questioning society and our role in it. What did it mean to be an American citizen during these years and afterward? What did it mean to be a man, a woman, a husband, a wife? Was marriage and the family still sacred and was God really dead, as *Time* magazine had asked?

The authors examined in this volume took up the challenge of these and other questions, sorting through them in an attempt to help themselves and their readers find the answers. The student can thus turn to Eudora Welty, Saul Bellow, or John Updike to learn the complicated politics of love, marriage, and relationships in the modern world; to Jack Kerouac, Kurt Vonnegut, or James Baldwin for an understanding of how much society has changed and to what degree those changes have affected who we are today; to J. D. Salinger for a nostalgic embrace of childhood innocence; to Flannery O'Connor and Updike, once again, for an incisive look at the value of religion in contemporary culture.

These writers and their works have very much been a product of the age, and as such may be appreciated not only for their artfulness but for how much they have contributed to the advancement of American letters. Some, like Kerouac or Vonnegut, successfully challenged conventional literary form and created new standards. Others, like Salinger, O'Connor, or Updike, relied on more traditional models but at the same time created stories with characters and situations which, just 20 years earlier, no mainstream publisher would have considered printing.

The authors profiled in this volume produced some of the best American fiction of the past half century. It could be said that they laid the foundation for contemporary American literature, but without question they had help—help from the likes of Truman Capote, John Cheever, Norman Mailer, Bernard Malamud, William Styron, Philip Roth, Raymond Carver, Tom Wolfe, Tom Robbins, Susan Minot, Alice Walker, and Toni Morrison,* to name but a few.

---

*See *Women Writers* in the American Profiles series for more information on Morrison and Walker.

Despite their differences in background and literary style, the writers in this book all share one single important influence. All of these authors spent hours of their formative years reading books they found in libraries, from the grandeur of the New York Public Library to the hushed and humble aisles of the local library in Jackson, Mississippi, that now bears Eudora Welty's name.

This book attempts to introduce the reader to the lives of these writers and to provide a small measure of insight into their work. A fuller understanding can be gained by visiting your school or local library and reading those works themselves.

Eudora Welty
(1909–   )

"Southern gentlewoman" Eudora Welty *has also
been called one of the best, if not* the best,
*American short-story writers of the twentieth
century. The last of the great Southern
Renaissance writers, her tales of families and
relationships have endured the test of time.*
(Library of Congress)

*I*n an era rocked by turbulent social, artistic, and political change, the life and career of Eudora Welty have ticked quietly and steadily along, like a trustworthy grandfather clock in one of the stately old southern homes of her fiction.

Born and raised in Jackson, Mississippi, where she has humbly spent the majority of her long life "underfoot locally," as she once put it, Welty has garnered some of the most prestigious and enviable honors any American writer could hope for, including the Pulitzer Prize, the National Medal for Literature, and the Presidential Medal of Freedom. She has strode with many of the literary giants of the Southern Renaissance such as William Faulkner, Katherine Anne Porter, and Robert Penn Warren. And while she has been praised as one of the best, if not *the* best, American short story writers of the twentieth century, she nevertheless "wears her celebrity like an invisible cloak," as journalist Sally Jacobs observed in a 1992 profile for *The Boston Globe:* "[T]here is a remarkable graciousness to Eudora Welty . . . [She is] a Southern gentlewoman to the core . . ."

The eldest of three children, Eudora Alice Welty was born on April 13, 1909, in Jackson, where her parents, Christian Webb and Mary Chestina (Andrews) Welty, had settled after their marriage five years earlier. Christian Welty was a Yankee from Ohio and Chestina (or Chessie, as she was called) came from West Virginia; both families had been in America since before the Revolution.

Christian Welty was a good-natured, practical man who ran a large insurance company based in Jackson. He shared with young Eudora his love of train travel, attention to detail, and, later, his well-intentioned reservations about her ever achieving "financial success by becoming a writer," as she recalled in her memoir, *One Writer's Beginnings* (1984). He nonetheless gave Welty her first dictionary, a Webster's Collegiate ("I still consult it," claimed Welty in 1984), and her first typewriter, a "little red Royal Portable."

But it was her mother, Welty recalls, who "emotionally and imaginatively supported" her desire to become a writer. A former schoolteacher, Chessie began by encouraging Eudora to read as much and as often as possible.

"I learned from age two or three that any room in our house, at any time of day, was there to read in, or be read to," recalls

2

Eudora Welty

Welty's birthplace in Jackson, Mississippi, where during her childhood every "room . . . was there to read in, or be read to." With the exception of a few years spent at college, Welty has lived her whole life in Jackson, finding plenty to write about in her own backyard. Today she lives in another house nearby.
(Courtesy of Mississippi Department of Archives and History)

Welty in *Beginnings.* "My mother read to me . . . in the big bedroom in the mornings, when we were in her rocker together . . . in the dining room on winter afternoons in front of the coal fire . . . in the kitchen while she sat churning [butter] . . . and at night when I'd got in my own bed. I must have given her no peace."

Books were revered and in evidence everywhere in the Welty household. In addition to the well-worn sets of Dickens, Stevenson, Scott, and Twain in the living room, there were "encyclopedia tables and [a] dictionary stand under [the] windows in [the] diningroom," as Welty recalled, to both instigate and settle suppertime debates.

The local public library (now named for Welty) was another important resource, and Welty's mother insisted that her daughter have her own library card at age nine. Chessie informed the fearful and monarchical old librarian, Mrs. Calloway—who used to send little girls back home to change clothes before issuing them a book if she thought they were improperly dressed—that young Eudora had "permission to read any book she wants from the shelves, children or adult."

This early exposure to the written word helped to cultivate in Welty a sensitivity to an "inward" voice, "the voice of the story or the poem itself," as she observed in *Beginnings*. Voices and language, both Welty's and those of her fabulous characters, are what contribute to the high art of her fiction. She grew up listening—to the hum of the water cooler in her father's office, to the busy gossip of the ladies who came to call, to the colorful stories that twined about her family tree—and incorporated what she heard into her stories. Writing "by ear," she once noted, always came easier to her. As scholar Ruth M. Vande Kieft observed, Welty "surrenders to the sound of her characters' speaking voices . . ." "Why I Live at the P.O.," "Petrified Man," and "A Memory" are but a few fine examples of this technique; all three stories appeared in Welty's first book, a short-story collection entitled *A Curtain of Green and Other Stories* (1941).

Wishing to leave her hometown for a while after graduating from high school in 1925, Welty enrolled at the Mississippi State College for Women, two hundred miles north of Jackson. She became a reporter and humor columnist for her campus newspaper, *The Spectator*, and enjoyed her first exposure to "what differences in background, persuasion of mind, and resources of character there were among Mississippians . . ."

After two years at MSCW, Welty transferred to the University of Wisconsin, a school with a strong liberal arts curriculum. There she expanded her literary horizons by delving into the great Russian novelists, as well as Yeats, Virginia Woolf, Faulkner, and other moderns of the day. She graduated with a bachelor of arts degree in 1929.

Eudora Welty

Teaching was the typical career choice for educated women in those days, but Welty had no desire to work in a classroom. (She "lacked . . . the patience," as she put it.) Knowing that she needed some practical experience to get a job, she spent the next two years in New York City studying advertising at Columbia University's Graduate School of Business. There were no advertising jobs to be had, however, once the Great Depression struck, and so Welty returned to Jackson in 1931. Later that year, her father died of leukemia.

Welty worked at a radio station for several years and freelanced for local newspapers to support herself. In 1933 she got her first full-time job as a publicity agent for the Works Progress Administration (WPA). The WPA was part of the "New Deal," President Roosevelt's economic recovery plan for the nation struggling to pull itself out of the Great Depression. Her job was to tour Mississippi, taking photographs of and interviewing people who were working on various WPA projects, such as rebuilding roads and towns, working with troubled youths, or rejuvenating farmlands. The job lasted three years and the experience, as Welty once commented, was "a revelation." Traversing "the whole of Mississippi," as she notes in *Beginnings*, " . . . I saw my home state at close hand, really for the first time."*

Many of the images that she caught on film became engraved in her mind as well—the rural families living in shacks, the dusty roadside county fairs, the tired towns. Photography taught her to always be on the lookout for just the right instant to click the shutter before the moment slipped away. Life was filled with such "crucial moment[s]" waiting to be captured, and this realization solidified her commitment to writing: "I felt the need to hold transient life in *words* . . . strongly enough to last me as long as I lived."

Welty published her first story, "Death of a Traveling Salesman," in 1936, the same year her job with the WPA ended. A friend had suggested she send some of her stories to John Rood, editor of a small literary magazine, *Manuscript*, publish-

---

*Welty's photographs were eventually published in a book entitled *One Time, One Place* (1971).

5

ed in Athens, Ohio. Rood accepted "Death of a Traveling Salesman" and "Magic" (1936), and informed Welty that they were two of the best stories he had ever read. *Manuscript* could not afford to pay its contributors, but Rood assured Welty that many reputable publishers scanned its pages in search of new talent. She was in too much awe over having been accepted to mind much about not being paid. Nevertheless, the publication of "Death of a Traveling Salesman," as scholar Elizabeth Evans notes, "was the modest launching of a great career."

Critics continue to praise "Death of a Traveling Salesman" as one of Welty's finest stories. Perhaps one reason for its enduring popularity is that it contains many of the hallmarks of Welty's fiction for which she has become noted, such as the family, rural settings, the complexities of relationships, isolation, and the human need for love.

R. J. Bowman is the ailing "traveling salesman" of the story who becomes lost on a country road, runs his car into a ditch, and is helped by a rural couple who live on a deserted hillside in a crude cabin. The husband, Sonny, uses ropes and a mule to rescue Bowman's car while the wife prepares a simple meal for them all. Feeling weak, the salesman asks if he can stay until morning and the couple obliges.

During his night's stay, Bowman becomes increasingly troubled, both physically and emotionally. He feels his heart begin "to behave strangely," beating in "uneven patterns" that practically paralyze his thoughts and ability to communicate. He is nonetheless desperate to do so. Touched by the couple's hospitality, Bowman becomes deeply moved when he discovers that the woman is pregnant: "He was shocked with knowing what was really in this house. A marriage, a fruitful marriage. That simple thing. Anyone could have had that." Yet the lonely, rootless nature of his job has denied him this "simple" experience and he finds himself wishing "that the child were his."

He is driven out of the house in the middle of the night by the sound of the couple breathing in the next room and the force of his own heart beating beneath his ribs. "[B]eautifully ready for love," as Vande Kieft put it, the salesman hopes for another chance at life, but before he can reach his car he has a heart attack, collapses in the road, and dies.

Welty's own comments on the importance of having roots (as quoted by Vande Kieft) perhaps best summarize the meaning behind Bowman's desperation and death: "Being on the move is no substitute for feeling. Nothing is. And no love or insight can be at work in a shifting and never-defined position . . . " Writing this particular story, Welty later observed, "opened [her] eyes" to her "real subject: human relationships."

The publication of "Death of a Traveling Salesman," as *Manuscript*'s John Rood had predicted, soon attracted the attention of other editors, not least among whom were Robert Penn Warren and Cleanth Brooks of *The Southern Review*, a journal dedicated to southern writing. Between 1937 and 1939, six of Welty's stories appeared in the journal, among them "A Memory," "A Curtain of Green," and "Petrified Man."

Warren and Brooks, in turn, introduced Welty's work to others, such as John Woodburn, an editor at Doubleday, Doran. While on a scouting mission through the South in search of new talent, Woodburn visited Welty, on *The Southern Review's* recommendation, and left bearing a handful of stories. He showed some of these to literary agent Diarmuid Russell, whose enthusiasm for Welty's work resulted in sales to such prestigious national publications as the *Atlantic Monthly* and *Harper's Bazaar*. Welty's career was now well under way and she felt confident enough to give up her various odd jobs and dedicate herself soley to writing.

Thanks to Russell's "hard-headed persistence," as Welty recalled, and Woodburn's unswerving faith in her work, Doubleday published *A Curtain of Green and Other Stories* in 1941. It hadn't been easy to convince them to accept a book of short fiction, since publishers typically prefer to see novels first. This seemed to make little difference to the critics who were, in fact, quite generous with the praise. "Few contemporary books have ever impressed me quite as deeply as this book of stories," gushed the reviewer for *The New York Times*. "A fine writer and a distinguished book," was *The New Yorker*'s view.

Time was impressed with Welty's "clean, original prose style" and her ability to produce "sharp landscapes and atmosphere, details of costume, action and speech, with flashes of real brilliance" while the *Saturday Review of Literature* made this exceedingly accurate prediction: "[Welty] is an author who is bound to take her place with the best in the short story field . . . "

Perhaps the kindest words came from Katherine Anne Porter, an influential admirer who provided an introduction to the book. "These stories offer an extraordinary range of mood, pace, tone, and variety of material," wrote Porter, "[W]here external act and the internal voiceless life of the human imagination almost meet and mingle on the mysterious threshold between dream and waking, one reality refusing to admit or confirm the existence of the other . . . This is not easy to accomplish . . . and Miss Welty is so successful at it, it would seem her most familiar territory."

Porter's reference to the "mysterious threshold" in Welty's fiction was quite on the mark. In an essay entitled "How I Write," Welty disclosed that the human relationship "*is* a pervading and changing mystery" and that "[b]rutal or lovely, the mystery waits for people wherever they go, whatever extreme they run to." One of Welty's remarkable skills as a writer is the deceptively simple way in which she reveals these mysteries to the reader. Through the highly crafted use of setting, for example, or dialogue, she leads us down what appears at first to be a recognizable path that gradually metamorphosizes into the bizarre, the comic, the tragic.

So a lost motorist's rescue in "Death of a Traveling Salesman" becomes a high moment of epiphany in the face of death; a schoolgirl's idle daydreams on a beach in "A Memory" are suddenly shattered by the simple yet terrifying realization that the world outside of her imagination is one she cannot control; the ranting of a jealous sister in "Why I Live at the P.O." becomes a comic monologue as well as a study in paranoia and eccentric characters.

With the success of *A Curtain of Green*, Welty's editor John Woodburn urged her to produce a novel. A year later, *The*

Robber Bridegroom (1942) was published. This short book, set in eighteenth-century Mississippi, is about a young woman, Rosamond, who is kidnapped by a romantic and mysterious bandit. He conceals his identity from her by darkening his features with berry juice. She nevertheless falls in love with her captor until she cleans the juice from his face one night while he is asleep and discovers that he is only Jamie Lockhart, a hired man of her father's. Lockhart casts her aside when he finds that she too has lied about who she is. They eventually reunite, Lockhart becomes a wealthy merchant, and they end up living in "a beautiful house of marble and cypress wood" with a pair of "beautiful twins" and "all they wanted in the world."

Written in simple, fairy-tale-like prose, *The Robber Bridegroom* is essentially a retelling of the Cupid and Psyche myth;* the book also borrows liberally from Grimm's *Fairy Tales* in terms of plot, settings—even its title. Into this mix, Welty added a smattering of American folklore—Davy Crockett, Indians, frontiersmen, bandits, etc.

Thematically, the novel follows the trail of Welty's earlier writing. "[A]ll things are double," observes Rosamond's father, "and this should keep us from taking liberties with the outside world, and acting too quickly to finish things off." In other words, things are not always what they seem, and few have rivaled Welty for her skill at subtly yet effectively conveying this idea.

As Welty's popularity increased, so did her stature in the literary community. She received first-place O. Henry Awards in 1942 and 1943 for "The Wide Net" and "Livvie Is Back," respectively; during those years she was also supported by a Guggenheim Fellowship, followed by an American Academy of

---

*Cupid, the Roman god of love, falls in love with Psyche, a beautiful young woman. He visits her every night under cover of darkness but leaves before sunrise so that she never sees his face. One night her curiosity overcomes her and she holds a lamp above Cupid's head; a drop of oil from the lamp falls on his shoulder and he awakens and flees. Abandoned, Psyche endures numerous trials until she and Cupid are reunited and she is made a goddess.

Arts and Letters Award in 1944. They were the first of many honors yet to come.

Welty's relationship with her editor, John Woodburn, was a close one, and she followed him in 1943 to Harcourt Brace where her next collection of short fiction, *The Wide Net and Other Stories* (1943), was published. In this book, Welty explores the shadowy world of dreams through use of myth, fantasy, the Gothic tradition, and even the resurrection of historical figures, such as Aaron Burr and John James Audubon. With the opening line of the first story, "First Love," Welty advises the reader to be prepared for something unusual: "Whatever happened, it happened in extraordinary times, in a season of dreams . . ."

The critics weren't quite sure what to make of *The Wide Net,* as it seemed so vastly different from *A Curtain of Green.* It remains Welty's least popular volume, although several of the stories—the award winners, "Livvie" (originally "Livvie Is Back") and the title story, as well as "At the Landing"—are considered among her best pieces of short fiction.

Welty's next novel, *Delta Wedding* (1946), began as a short story, the unpublished "Delta Cousins," which her agent, Diarmuid Russell, returned with a note attached: "This is chapter two of a novel." Russell immediately recognized that the boisterous, teeming, and infectiously charming Fairchild clan and its assorted hangers-on needed much more elbow room than the short-story format could provide. His intuition resulted in one of Welty's most memorable books.

Set in 1923—a year which Welty chose specifically because it had been free of natural disaster in the Mississippi Delta and there were no wars of significance raging abroad so that there could be plenty of male characters on hand—the story concerns events leading up to a wedding at the Shellmound plantation, ancestral sod of the Fairchilds.

Welty has denied that the book is a portrait of traditional southern plantation society; nevertheless, her vivid and ample descriptions of life among the Fairchilds, such as a typical dinner, provide us with a window into a world that was no doubt familiar to her: "They had been eating chicken and ham and dressing and gravy, and good, black snap beans, greens, butter beans, okra, corn on the cob, all kinds of relish, and watermelon rind preserves, and that good bread . . ."

The characters in the novel recognize the power and importance of family in their lives, "[t]hus the end of the action," notes scholar J. A. Bryant, "is the vindication of that family bond—mysterious, compelling, and in the final reckoning good . . ."

Families, once again, provide the dramatic backdrop for Welty's ongoing exploration of human relationships in her next collection of short fiction, *The Golden Apples* (1949). These stories track the comings and goings of several different clans over a forty-year span in the fictitious town of Morgana, Mississippi.

The title comes from Greek mythology and refers to the treasured golden apples that grew in a garden tended by the Hesperides, daughters of Atlas. These apples symbolized immortality and perfection and the desire for them often resulted in misfortune or regret. A golden apple was the initial cause of the Trojan War, brought about the downfall of Atalanta and Hippomenes, and, in Celtic myth, doomed the youthful god Aengus to an endless search of beauty.[*]

Like their mythological counterparts—Hercules, Ulysses, Perseus—many of the book's major characters are adventurers whose journeys often bring them into conflict with and force

---

[*]Angered because she was the only deity not invited to the wedding of Thetis and Peleus, Eris, goddess of discord, appears at the feast bearing a golden apple inscribed with the words "For the fairest" and tosses it among the guests. Hera, Athene, and Aphrodite all claim the apple and appeal to Zeus for judgment, but he wisely declines and appoints the handsomest man in the world, Paris of Troy, as judge. Paris awards the apple to Aphrodite, who had promised him, as a reward, that he could have the most beautiful woman on earth, Helen, wife of King Menelaus of Sparta. Paris abducts Helen and returns to Troy pursued by all the kings of Greece, who lay siege to the city in honor of their promise to Menelaus that they would come to his aid if ever Helen was harmed.

In the story of Atalanta and Hippomenes, Atalanta is a beautiful, athletic young woman who has vowed never to wed, fearing the prophesy that marriage would prove fatal. She devises a scheme to rid herself of her many suitors by challenging them to a footrace: the winner to have her hand, the losers to be

them to face their own limitations. Loneliness, as scholar Elizabeth Evans points out, is the dominant theme of the book, together with "the unsuccessful search for love, the urge to wander, the mystery of human life, [and] the disparity between expectation and fulfillment." Many of the characters in these stories are "like lost beasts," muses Cassie Morrison in "June Recital," "roaming on the face of the earth" while their dreams of fulfillment, suggests scholar Vande Kieft, may be nothing more than illusion, a fata morgana[*], or mirage, as the name of the town implies.

While some critics have suggested that *The Golden Apples* is best read as a novel, Welty has steadfastly maintained such is not the case. One scholar suggests that, like the ancient myths, the stories may form a cycle. Whatever its genre, the book continues to be one of Welty's most critically studied works. Welty herself, as quoted by Evans, has described the collection as "the closest to my heart of all my books."

Welty revisited her gift for comic monologue with her next novel, *The Ponder Heart* (1954). Its narrator, Miss Edna Earle Ponder, chronicles the daily trials and tribulations of the residents of the fictional town of Clay, Mississippi. Her story focuses particularly on the romantic misadventures of her twice-married Uncle Daniel Ponder, who inherits a fortune and

---

put to death. One by one, the suitors lose and are executed until Hippomenes accepts the challenge. Calling upon the goddess Aphrodite for help, Hippomenes receives from her three golden apples and throws these in Atalanta's path during the race. Tempted, Atalanta bends to pick up the apples and loses the contest. She is actually happy to wed Hippomenes, but the couple forgets to thank Aphrodite for her intervention and the offended goddess turns the lovers into chariot-pulling lions.

Aengus, a Celtic hero-god associated with beauty and poetry, catches a silver trout that suddenly changes into a beautiful girl with apple blossoms in her hair. She calls his name before vanishing and he spends the rest of his days searching for her so that he may "pluck . . . The golden apples of the sun" as poet William Butler Yeats wrote in "The Song of the Wandering Aengus." Welty quotes from the poem in one of the stories, "June Recital."

[*]Literally the fairy Morgan (from the Italian *fata*, fairy), or Morgan le Fay, the sorceress of Arthurian legend who sealed Merlin in a cave for all time by tricking him with her witchcraft—yet another example of Welty's use of mythology in the book.

is accused of murdering his estranged second wife, Bonnie Dee Peacock, by tickling her to death with a tassel. "She was dead as a doornail. And she's died laughing," reports Edna Earle. Welty's masterful use of southern idiomatic speech, colorful characters, and absurd situations in *The Ponder Heart* have inspired many to consider the book her comic masterpiece. The novel was dramatized in 1956 and became an award-winning Broadway hit.

After publishing *The Bride of the Innisfallen and Other Stories* (1955), Welty dropped out of the public view for the next fifteen years, primarily to take care of her ailing mother, who died in 1966. Never a politically motivated writer, she had little to add to the volcanic cultural and social discourse of the sixties. She made an exception in July of 1963 with "Where Is the Voice Coming From?", a piece for *The New Yorker* expressing outrage over the murder of black civil rights activist and Jackson resident Medgar Evers.

During these years, she also added to scholarship by producing several books on fiction (*Place in Fiction* [1957], *Three Papers on Fiction* [1962]) as well as numerous articles such as "Is There a Reader in the House?", "And They All Lived Happily Ever After," and "English from the Inside" for such publications as *Mississippi Educational Advance*, *The New York Times Book Review*, and *American Education*.

In 1970, Welty broke her lengthy artistic silence with her longest novel to date, *Losing Battles*. Though the action of the book only takes place over the course of two days, Welty manages to broaden its sweep to include four generations of families in the Depression-era community of Banner, Mississippi. Two dozen or more friends and relatives of the Beecham and Renfro families gather to celebrate "Granny" Elvira Jordan Vaughn's ninetieth birthday. All have their tales to tell of growing up in Banner and this draws the action of the novel out to over 400 pages.

Many of these fables include memories of the old schoolteacher, Miss Julia Mortimer ("Solid as a rock and not one bit of nonsense, looking like the Presbyterian she started out to be.") and of her efforts to educate the populace of Banner while providing them with food and comfort during hard times. Miss Julia's struggles are some of the lost battles of the book, which is nonetheless comic in spirit, thanks to characters like the tactlessly inquisitive Aunt Cleo or episodes of physical comedy approaching slapstick.

Losing Battles was the first of Welty's books to reach the bestseller list. Rich in detail, eccentric characters, and amusing situations, the novel, notes scholar Elizabeth Evans, is "an expression of Welty's persistent emphasis on the mystery of human relationships and on the redeeming power of love."

Over the years, Welty continued to receive accolades and awards from the literary establishment—another Guggenheim in 1949–50, which allowed her to travel to Europe, election to the National Institute of Arts and Letters in 1952, the William Dean Howells Medal of the Academy of Arts and Letters (of which she became a member in 1971) for *The Ponder Heart*, 1955, and the Gold Medal for Fiction in 1972. There were also numerous fellowships and lecture seats at England's Cambridge University, Bryn Mawr College, as well as a professorship at Smith College. In 1973, she received a Pulitzer Prize, an honor which many said was long overdue.

Welty's Pulitzer was awarded for her last novel to date, *The Optimist's Daughter* (1972). The story of a daughter's painful self-examination in the wake of her father's death, this short novel, as Evans notes, explores many of Welty's familiar topics—family, community, social structures, marriage, loneliness, and the enduring support that love provides. To the daughter, Laurel McKelva, it is the memory of love that moves us to despair, yet furnishes us with strength:

> *It is memory that is the somnambulist. It will come back in its wounds from across the world . . . calling us by our names and demanding its rightful tears. It will never be impervious. The memory can be hurt, time and again—but in that may lie its final mercy. As long as it's vulnerable to the living moment, it lives for us, and while it lives, and while we are able, we can give it up its due.*

Eudora Welty

Welty continued to publish several essays and lectures throughout the seventies. In 1980, Harcourt Brace Jovanovich released *The Collected Stories of Eudora Welty,* for which she penned a preface. "If [my stories] have any special virtue," she wrote, "it would lie in the fact that they . . . are stories written from within. They come from living here [in Jackson]—they were *part* of living here, of my long familiarity with the thoughts and feelings of those around me, in their many shadings and variations and contradictions."

In 1984, by which time the publishing world may have expected Welty to rest and retire on the well-deserved laurels of a long and fruitful career, she surprised and delighted audiences with one of her most popular books, *One Writer's Beginnings,* a flawlessly crafted memoir (stitched together from a series of lectures at Harvard University) in which she once again underscored the importance of the writer's inward journey: "I am a writer who came of a sheltered life. A sheltered life can be a daring life as well. For all serious daring starts from within."

Welty continues to live by herself, in a large, Tudor-style house in Jackson where devoted admirers occasionally show up and ring her doorbell. Ever the southern gentlewoman, Welty is courteous to such pilgrims, even though she once confessed to a reporter, "I don't want to carry on, but I don't really like it."

Among the last of the great Southern Renaissance writers, Welty remains one of modern American literature's greatest treasures. While the subject of numerous critical studies, Welty's fiction hardly requires the validating stamp of academic approval to prove its merit, as Robert Penn Warren once observed. "[T]he work, at its best," he wrote, "is so fully created, so deeply realized, and formed with such apparent innocence that it offers only itself, in shining unity."

Chronology

—————

April 13, 1909	born in Jackson, Mississippi
1925–29	attends Mississippi State College for Women for two years; writes for campus newspaper, *The Spectator*; transfers to University of Wisconsin and graduates with a bachelor of arts degree, class of '29
1929–31	attends Columbia University's Graduate School of Business; returns to Jackson for good in 1931; father dies of leukemia same year
1933–36	works as a publicity agent for the Works Progress Administration (WPA); publishes first story, "Death of a Traveling Salesman" (1936) in *Manuscript*
1941	*A Curtain of Green and Other Stories*, first book, a critical success
1943	*The Wide Net and Other Stories*; receives first-place O. Henry Award for "Livvie Is Back"
1946	*Delta Wedding*
1949–50	*The Golden Apples* (1949); travels to Europe on a Guggenheim fellowship
1952	elected to the National Institute of Arts and Letters
1955–66	devotes majority of time to caring for sick mother, who dies in 1966
1970	*Losing Battles* becomes best-seller

Eudora Welty

1973 receives Pulitzer Prize for *The Optimist's Daughter* (1972)
1980 *The Collected Stories of Eudora Welty*
1984 *One Writer's Beginnings*

Further Reading

Welty's Works

Delta Wedding (New York: Harcourt, Brace & World, Inc., 1946). Welty's warm and comic novel of family life in the Deep South during the twenties.

The Collected Stories of Eudora Welty (New York: Harcourt Brace Jovanovich, 1980). Complete collected works of short fiction, plus the previously uncollected pieces "Where Is the Voice Coming From?" and "The Demonstrators."

The Optimist's Daughter (New York: Random House, 1972). Welty's Pulitzer Prize–winning novel which *The Philadelphia Inquirer* called a "masterpiece of American fiction."

One Writer's Beginnings (Cambridge, Massachusetts: Harvard University Press, 1984). Welty's warm and insightful exploration of the seeds of her career as a writer.

Books About Welty

J. A. Bryant, Jr., *Eudora Welty* (Minneapolis: University of Minnesota Press, 1968). Concise, critical overview of Welty's major works and stories up until 1968. No. 66 in the University of Minnesota Pamphlets on American Writers series.

Elizabeth Evans, *Eudora Welty* (New York: Frederick Ungar Publishing Co., 1981). Well-researched critical biography. Includes bibliography and chronology.

Michael Kreyling, *Author and Agent: Eudora Welty and Diarmuid Russell* (New York: Farrar, Straus and Giroux, 1991). Thirty years of correspondence forms the backbone of this look at Russell's warm and supportive relationship with his client. Provides insights into the changing dynamics of the publishing world, Welty's work habits, and the rise of Southern literature.

Ruth M. Vande Kieft, *Eudora Welty* (New York: Twayne Publishers, Inc., 1962). Provides extensive analysis of the major works until 1962.

Saul Bellow
(1915–)

Saul Bellow, winner of both the Nobel and Pulitzer Prizes, has been called America's "premier novelist." His blend of Jewish wit and impressive scholarly knowledge have added richness and depth to his works, which chronicle an urban America in transition.
(National Archives)

"*I* am an American, Chicago born . . . and go at things as I have taught myself, free-style, and will make the record in my own way . . ." declares the titular hero of *The Adventures of Augie March* (1953), Saul Bellow's masterful third novel and the book that effectively launched his career. *Augie March* is a book that cut its own path through the landscape of American culture in the earlier decades of this century.

"[L]oose in form and extravagant in language," (as scholar Robert Kiernan observed), the novel typifies the breadth and richness of Bellow's America, a world of dramatic cityscapes and suburban jungles populated by roguish immigrants and boisterous millionaires. Bellow's sweeping look at our modern civilization, his remarkable command of various cultural and intellectual sources, and his consistently impressive output over the years have made him one the country's preeminent writers—the literary heir of Faulkner, Hemingway, and Fitzgerald.

This man, whom the *New York Times Book Review* has called "the premier American novelist" of our day is actually of Canadian origin, born Solomon Bellow (not "Saul" until he started publishing) on June 10, 1915, in Lachine, an impoverished suburb of Montreal, Quebec. He was the fourth child of Abraham and Liza (Gordon) Bellow, well-off Russian Jews who fell on hard times and emigrated from St. Petersburg two years earlier. Abraham Bellow, an importer and sometime bootlegger, settled in Montreal's Rachel Market section—a teeming ethnic slum, rich in western European Jewish culture, where Hebrew was the language of school and synagogue and Yiddish the dialect of the home and street.

Weaned on the Old Testament, Bellow could recite biblical passages from memory at age four. Although in later years he would resist the label of "Jewish writer," the genealogies of such characters as Moses Herzog and Augie March could almost certainly be traced back, in part, to the ethnic neighborhood of his youth.

In 1924 the family moved to Chicago, the city which Bellow considered home and with which he is most often identified. During the early decades of the century, Chicago was a true melting pot: "The neighborhood was largely Polish and Ukrainian, Swedish, Catholic, Orthodox, and Evangelical Lutheran," relates Bellow/the narrator in the short story, "Zetland: By a

Character Witness" (1974).[*] "The Jews were few and the streets were tough. Bungalows and brick three-flats were the buildings. Back stairs and porches were made of crude gray lumber . . . The heat was corrosive, and the cold like a guillotine as you waited for the streetcar."

The Chicago of this day "was a good town for novelists to grow up in," observed critic Alfred Kazin in a 1965 *Atlantic Monthly* article entitled "My Friend Saul Bellow." "Much of the vividness of Bellow's novels, his powerful sense of place, comes out of Chicago" of the twenties and thirties, with its bustling and congested streets, clamorous slaughterhouses, and mighty towers of commerce.

Like most inner-city kids of the time, Bellow played stickball in the streets and loitered on tenement steps with his pals. Yet he also spent a lot of his free time in the public library, and by high school had read his way through many of the great Americans, such as James Fenimore Cooper, Edgar Allan Poe, Mark Twain, O. Henry, Jack London, Sherwood Anderson, and Theodore Dreiser. He and several classmates shared aspirations of becoming great writers and met regularly to discuss books and read each other's stories.

Upon graduation from high school in 1933, Bellow continued his literary pursuits at the University of Chicago but soon discovered that the formal study of literature was not for him. "My tastes and habits were those of a writer," he reported fifty years later in his foreword to Allan Bloom's *The Closing of the American Mind*. "Registering for a poetry course, I was soon bored by meters and stanzas . . . I preferred to read poetry on my own without the benefit of lectures on the caesura." This was just as well, as the English department chairman had regretfully warned him that anti-Semitism in the upper levels of academia could block his scholarly career.

Transferring to Northwestern University, he earned an honors degree in sociology and anthropology in 1937. He accepted a scholarship to the University of Wisconsin, where he began

---

[*] Later collected in *Him With His Foot in His Mouth and Other Stories* (1984).

work on his master's degree in anthropology, but quit by Christmas. One of his professors had gently advised against a career in science. Bellow's writing, said the professor, had too much style—every scientific thesis he attempted ended up as a story. Details that Bellow picked up in his studies of various African tribes, however, would later come in handy when writing his comic masterpiece *Henderson the Rain King* (1959).

Returning to Chicago at age 22, determined to be a writer, Bellow married Anita Goshkin and struggled to make ends meet, living "on what might be called the literary fringe," as scholar Peter Hyland put it in his 1992 study *Saul Bellow*. He was just scraping by on about fifty dollars a week writing book reviews (supplementing his income by selling the books to a used bookstore after he read them) when he was lucky enough to find work with the Writers Project of the Works Progress Administration. Part of President Franklin D. Roosevelt's plan, or "New Deal," to pull the nation out of the depths of the Depression, Bellow's job for the Writer's Project was to write biographies of midwestern authors. "I suppose the intention really was to keep the bums out of trouble and to prevent them from joining subversive organizations," he later said of his government work.

In 1938, Bellow began his long-standing association with academia by taking a teaching job at Pestalozzi-Froebel Teachers' College in Chicago. Teaching was (and remains) a typical career path and means of support for many writers, and in later years Bellow would teach at various institutions, most notably at the University of Chicago. During Bellow's four years at Pestalozzi-Froebel, his first son, Gregory, was born, and his first published short story, "Two Morning Monologues" (1941), appeared in the *Partisan Review*. The *Review* was a prestigious literary publication whose circle of artists included friend, poet, and critic Delmore Schwartz, whom Bellow would later lovingly portray as Von Humboldt Fleisher, the tragic poet hero of *Humboldt's Gift* (1975).

Bellow left his next job—in the editorial department of the *Encyclopaedia Brittanica*—to work, briefly, in the merchant marine during World War II. He never saw any action from the relative comfort of Sheepshead Bay in Brooklyn, New York, where he was assigned, but his experiences provided material for his first novel, *The Dangling Man* (1944), the story of a young Chicagoan who sits out the war waiting to be called to active duty.

The book received considerable critical acclaim. Delmore Schwartz, in the pages of the *Partisan Review*, hailed Bellow as the first writer to capture the spirit of his age while the esteemed critic Edmund Wilson praised *The Dangling Man* as a "testimony on the psychology" of a generation that came of age during the Depression and the war. Bellow followed up his success with *The Victim* (1947), a story of anti-Semitism set in Manhattan. Once more, the reviews were favorable (some compared him to the great Russian novelist Fyodor Dostoyevski) and Bellow's writing career was under way.

From 1948 to 1950, Bellow lived in Paris, supported by a Guggenheim Fellowship. He toured Europe extensively and "got used to writing on the roll," as he later recalled, composing his third book, *Augie March*, on trains and in cafés. Upon his return to the States he took a teaching job at New York University and settled in Manhattan where he became identified with the *Partisan Review* as well as a crowd of young and promising American Jewish writers, among them Norman Mailer, Bernard Malamud, J. D. Salinger, and Philip Roth. Bellow, however, has always resisted the label, "American Jewish writer": "It is accurate only insofar as it is true that I am an American and a Jew and a writer," he once told the *New York Times Book Review*.

Soon after Bellow's return to the States, he left New York for Princeton, armed with a creative writing fellowship and a National Institute of Arts and Letters grant. The time and money helped him to complete *Augie March*, which was published in 1953.

The hero of this rambling book is Augie March, who, like Bellow, is a Depression-era Chicago native who does odd jobs to make a living, travels abroad, joins the merchant marine, and marries. But unlike Bellow, who knew what he wanted to do in life, Augie drifts from place to place and career to career, attaching himself to various mentors along the way on a journey of self-discovery.

Although in the final chapter Augie is still optimistic, and speaks of himself as "a laughing creature, forever rising up," the subtle truth is that after having declined the various offers from others, he has in essence cut himself loose from humanity. He is empty inside, a "man with no commitments," as Robert Penn Warren observed.

Augie March succeeds for various reasons, not the least of which is the richness of Bellow's narrative. "Sentences both nimble and zestful sweep down the page with a sense of release from conventional linguistic decorum . . . [a]s if the workaday language were not adequate for all that Augie has to say," noted scholar Robert Kiernan. Bellow's sensual language and descriptive powers significantly contribute to the texture and identity of the novel:

> *I took pleasure in sitting in the still green bake of the Civil War courthouse square after my thick breakfast of griddle cakes and eggs and coffee . . . The benches were white iron, roomy enough for three or four old gaffers to snooze on in the swamp-tasting sweet warmth that made the redwing blackbirds fierce and quick, and the flowers frill, but other living things slow and lazy-blooded. I soaked in the heavy nourishing air and this befriending atmosphere like rich life-cake, the kind that encourages love and brings on a mild pain of emotions.*

Bellow also frequently employs the literary device of the catalogue to set his scenes. Thus, riding in the elevator of Chicago's gritty City Hall, one often "rub[bed] elbows with bigshots and operators, commissioners, grabbers, heelers, tipsters, hoodlums, wolves, fixers, plaintiffs, flatfeet, men in Western hats and women in lizard shoes and fur coats . . ."; the Lake Michigan resort where his benefactors, the Renlings, take Augie is characterized by "greenery and wickerwork, braid cord on the portieres, menus in French, white hall runners and deep fat of money, limousines in the washed gravel, lavish culture of flowers bigger than life, and triple-decker turf on which the grass lived rich."

Bellow is indebted for his use of catalogue to the great nineteeth-century American poet Walt Whitman. Numerous critics and scholars, in fact, have compared the language and plot of *Augie March* to Whitman's classic, *Leaves of Grass*. As scholar Peter Hyland observed, *Augie March*, like *Leaves*, is about self-discovery: "I celebrate myself, and sing myself/And what I assume you shall assume,/For every atom belonging to me as good belongs to you" are Whitman's famous opening lines in *Leaves;* Augie declares that he is "available to everybody . . . assuming about others what I assumed about myself." Where Whitman claims to be all Americans, "of every rank and religion" and occupation, Augie "experienc[es] American life on . . . many social levels," writes Hyland. "[B]oth are presented as the embodiment of American diversity."

Augie March, Bellow admits, also owes something to a classic literary form, the picaresque novel. The hero, or the "picaroon" (from *picaro*, Spanish for "rogue"), is typically a character of low birth and loose morals, forced to live by his wits. The picaresque author satirizes various social types whom the picaroon outfoxes in a series of unrelated adventures. While *Augie March* may partially fit this bill, the picaroon, as Hyland notes, is usually unchanged by his adventures; Bellow's book (as scholar Keith Opdahl has observed) may be closer to the German *Bildungsroman*, the "novel of education" which chronicles the personal development of a single individual from youth to maturity.*

Critics, in general, were not overly fond of *Augie March*. They thought the novel bloated and shapeless, Bellow's colloquialisms confusing, and his prose "over-enthusiastic" (as *Time* magazine put it). However, several respected members of the

---

*Familiar picaresque novels in Western literature include Cervantes' *Don Quixote*, Daniel Defoe's *Moll Flanders*, Henry Fielding's *Tom Jones* and Mark Twain's *The Adventures of Huckleberry Finn;* Thomas Mann's *The Magic Mountain* and Charles Dickens' *David Copperfield* are examples of the *Bildungsroman*.

literati, most notably Robert Penn Warren, recognized the book's virtues—its humor, the cleverness of its numerous literary and historical allusions (a Bellow trademark), and the distinctively American resiliency and pluck of Augie. "[F]rom now on," wrote Warren prophetically, "any discussion of fiction in America in our time will have to take account of [*The Adventures of Augie March*]." The committee for the National Book Award agreed and voted the novel the best book of 1953. This tribute was followed by a second Guggenheim in 1955 and a two-year Ford Foundation grant in 1959.

In the midst of these honors came an unhappy divorce from Anita in 1956, followed by a second marriage, to Alexandra Tachacbasoz with whom Bellow had another son, Adam. The author took a teaching job at Bard College and he and his family moved into "an old Faulkner mansion that had drifted north," as Bellow described it, on the Hudson River in Tivoli, New York.

Bellow's next major work, the novella *Seize the Day* (1956), concerns one day in the life of middle-aged Wilhelm Adler. Wilhelm is a sloppy, unemployed would-be actor who takes the stage name, Tommy Wilhelm, in a futile attempt to establish his career.

Through the course of the novel, Wilhelm sinks into a depression, which he is finally lifted out of when he turns his attention from himself and his troubles to another human being's suffering. In Wilhelm's compassion for another person, he experiences a small moral triumph. The critics of the day, however, saw little triumph in *Seize the Day;* in fact, they almost universally condemned the book. "Not literature," "slight," and "a small success" were some of the least derogatory remarks (as quoted by Ruth Miller in *Saul Bellow, A Biography of the Imagination*) of reviewers.

In the wake of these notices, Bellow began his now long-standing practice of defending his work (and that of fiction writers in general) by responding to his critics in print and in public. He disapproves of literary interpretation and considers the dissection of literature an offense to the artist and the reader, perpetrated by university English professors who are "in charge of masterpieces but not themselves inspired." Modern literary criticism, Bellow has charged, is driven by "publicity intellectuals"—those critics, academics, members of the press, and "middle-class bohemians of New York" who have "brought about the professionalization of culture." In a 1976 *New York Times* interview, he said this crowd reminded him of the "man who steps to center stage with his thumbs looped in his suspenders, giving off an air of tremendous confidence, as if to say, 'I've got the poop.' Well, as I see it, he doesn't have the poop, just the suspenders."

Bellow followed *Seize the Day* with what is considered his most comic novel, *Henderson the Rain King*. Eugene Henderson is an eccentric, late-middle-aged millionaire plagued by an inner voice that taunts him ("It only said one thing, *I want, I want!*"). Spurned by his now-deceased father, he abandons his family's Connecticut estate, which he has disrespectfully turned into a pig farm, and sets out for Africa in search of meaning in his life.

In *Henderson the Rain King*, Bellow's Africa is a fictitious one, derived from his graduate-school studies of African tribal cultures as well as the works of several authorities on the continent, such as the English explorer Sir Richard Burton. The book was criticized for its romanticized and mythical depiction of Africa and its people, but those who took issue with this may have been missing the point. *Henderson* is, among other things, a parody. The bungling, blustery, bigger-than-life Eugene Henderson is an exaggerated version of the classic and autobiographical Ernest Hemingway protagonist (they even share the same initials, E. H.). Like the stock Hemingway hero, Henderson exiles himself from society and hides his inner grief with bravado. The book is also a send-up of an ageless Western form, the quest epic/novel, in which the hero journeys into the wilderness and confronts its perils in search of an ideal or some embodiment of truth. As such, *Henderson* borrows liberally from numerous classics of quest literature, e.g., *Don Quixote, Moby Dick, Huckleberry Finn, Heart of Darkness,* and *The Catcher in the Rye.* Several of Bellow's fellow fiction writers, such as Bernard Malamud and Henry Miller, were kinder to *Henderson the Rain King* than the critics, and the esteemed academic Alfred Kazin clearly recognized the novel's value.

While Bellow's professional career was blossoming, his personal life was once more in turmoil. His marriage to Alexandra ended in divorce in 1960 and a year later he wedded Susan Glassman, with whom he had a third child, Daniel. After serving as a visiting professor at the University of Puerto Rico, Bellow returned to his home city to teach at the University of Chicago. More trouble followed when his marriage to Susan began to deteriorate after several years, ending in an ugly divorce in 1968 which was followed by a decade of bitter legal disputes over alimony. If nothing else, Bellow's disastrous marital experiences provided rich material for his later books, including *Herzog* (1964), which some consider to be his masterpiece.

The novel concerns several days in the tortured life of Moses Elkanah Herzog, a twice-divorced college professor living alone in a restored farmhouse that has gone to seed in the western hills of Massachusetts. "If I am out of my mind, it's all right with me," are Herzog's compelling first words to the reader—what follows is a ricocheting, five-day trek from Herzog's house in the Berkshire town of Ludeyville to Martha's Vineyard, to Chicago where he comes close to killing his ex-wife and her lover, then back to Massachusetts where he began.

Herzog's journey is at once external and internal. Throughout the course of his five-day odyssey, he reveals details about his past as well as insights into his character by way of his ruminations and the numerous letters, both real and imagined, which he composes at all hours of the day or night. These letters are addressed to a host of historical and fictional characters—from philosophers and politicians, both living and dead, to academicians, writers, theologians, *The New York Times,* himself, even to God.

The letters are the canvas upon which Herzog works through his search for order in his life: "Late in spring Herzog had been overcome by the need to explain, to have it out, to justify, to put into perspective, to clarify, to make amends." A common theme of these missives is the main character's disgust with the subjugation of private thoughts and emotions to intellectual scrutiny. "If the unexplained life is not worth living, the explained life is unbearable, too," the protagonist writes. According to scholar Robert Kiernan, the content of the letters also represents the difficulty of coordinating "intelligence and experience without dismissing the claims of either. Indeed, the pull of these assorted tensions is Bellow's point."

Other critics have viewed *Herzog* as a lament for the "disintegration of society" and as an expression of Bellow's "outrage at the betrayal of the immigrant's dream," as biographer Ruth Miller notes. Bellow "needed to understand" how Chicago, once the great city of opportunity for immigrants like his father, had become one of the most segregated, corrupt, and politically oppressive municipalities in the country—"threatening, duplicitous, faithless, like America." The novel reflects Bellow's frustration with recent events: How could four black college students be thrown in jail for ordering cups of coffee at a North Carolina lunch counter? Why did a concrete wall suddenly divide Germany? What did the U.S. hoped to accomplish in Vietnam?

Bellow was compared to Thomas Mann and James Joyce for the depth and complexity of the writing in *Herzog.* Many saw the novel as a fictional summing up of everything that Bellow had produced in the past. They also noted that it was his most thoroughly ethnic book to date, "full of Jewish wit, humor, pathos, intellectual and moral passion," according to the *Times* reviewer, who compared Moses Herzog to the Jews of his generation—"a survivor with the responsibility of testifying to the continued existence of values" that the Nazis had tried to stamp out in the Holocaust.

In 1965, Bellow received his second National Book Award as well as the prestigious Prix Littéraire International for *Herzog*. That year he also published his second play, *The Last Analysis*, which flopped on Broadway; the following year he took another unsuccessful stab at drama with three one-act plays (*Out from Under, Orange Soufflé,* and *A Wen*), collectively entitled *Under the Weather*.

Bellow turned to journalism two years later in 1967. In mid-June of that year, Israeli troops seized control of the Sinai Peninsula, Jerusalem, and other major Arab cities in what became known as the Six-Day War. Journalist Bill Moyers, then publisher of *Newsday*, dispatched Bellow to the Middle East to cover the conflict. Bellow's moving though somewhat controversial reports—reprinted in the nonfiction collection, *It All Adds Up* (1994)—emphasized the horrific brutality of war and questioned, rather than glorified, the victory, contrary to what many pro-Israeli readers back home might have expected.

"[I]t seems all wrong," Bellow summarized in his final report, dated June 16, 1967. "What good are these traditional dignities? No good at all if they lead to the Sinai roads with their blasted Russian tanks, the black faces of the dead dissolving, and the survivors fighting for a sip of ditch water."

Bellow received more accolades the following year—the Jewish Heritage Award from B'nai B'rith and the Croix de Chevalier des Arts et Lettres from the French government—while Viking released a collection of new and previously published short fiction, *Mosby's Memoirs and Other Stories*. In these stories, Bellow "combines an understanding of loneliness and despair with a sense of comedy," as *The New Yorker* put it. The collection also illustrates the author's increasingly masterful use of interior monologue.

Bellow won his third National Book Award for his next novel, *Mr. Sammler's Planet* (1970), the story of Artur Sammler, a Polish, Oxford-educated, Jewish intellectual and journalist, embittered by the Holocaust, in which he lost his wife and his sight in one eye. Rescued by his nephew, Dr. Elya Gruner,

Sammler and his daughter Shula are taken to New York where Sammler becomes a sort of misanthropic intellectual-at-large and lecturer at Columbia University, supposedly working on a book about his old Bloomsbury-days friend, writer H. G. Wells. Distressed, at first, by what he calls the "madness" of life in New York, with its pickpockets and radicals who heckle him in the lecture hall, Sammler comes to terms with life after Gruner's death.

Bellow came under considerable fire from the extreme left for *Mr. Sammler's Planet.* Published at the height of the anti–Vietnam War demonstrations on college campuses across the country, the book was viewed by many as an open attack on the protest movement. Like Sammler, Bellow had once been heckled at the college lecture podium, and didn't approve. In spite of what the more radical element on campus thought of him, however, those in authority were treating him with increasing respect and admiration. In 1970, he was made a fellow of the American Academy of Arts and Sciences while New York University bestowed upon him an honorary doctorate; two years later both Harvard and Yale followed suit.

In 1975, Alexandra Ionescu Tulcea, a Romanian-born professor of theoretical mathematics at Northwestern University, became the fourth and, to date, the last Mrs. Saul Bellow. Married life had, hitherto, not been very kind to Bellow. The divorce proceedings with his last wife, Susan, dragged on longer than their marriage and the various appeals, counterappeals, and ensuing settlement ate up most of the money he earned from *Herzog,* which had been a best-seller. As he had done in *Herzog,* however, Bellow incorporated these experiences into his fiction, and thus Charlie Citrine, the main character of his next and perhaps most accomplished novel, *Humboldt's Gift,* is harried by rapacious lawyers, unfair judges, alimony payments and shrewish wives.

Some critics trounced Bellow, finding every fault they could in *Humboldt's Gift,* from its "agitated sluggishness" (John Updike for *The New Yorker*), to its "well-trod" theme (Daniel Aaron for *The New Republic*), to the regrettable supposition that the book fell far short of its author's "awaited masterpiece" (Roger Shattuck in *The New York Review of Books*).

Once more, however, Bellow had the final word when *Humboldt's Gift* won the 1976 Pulitzer Prize for fiction, followed by the Swedish Academy's decision to award him the Nobel Prize for Literature, making him the first American to be so honored since John Steinbeck in 1962. In that same remarkable year, Bellow also became the first man of letters to receive a Legacy Award from the Anti-Defamation League of B'nai B'rith, whose previous honorees included Presidents Dwight D. Eisenhower and John F. Kennedy, Eleanor Roosevelt, and Adlai Stevenson. A Gold Medal for the Novel from the American Academy of Arts and Letters capped this remarkable period of recognition for Bellow. "How many American writers have published first-rate, imaginative books over a 30-year period?" asked *The New York Times Magazine* in a November 1976 profile. Their answer: "Perhaps three, Henry James, Faulkner and now Bellow." Not bad company for a poor Jewish kid from the slums of Quebec.

In a painfully familiar pattern, however, the complications of Bellow's personal life clouded his artistic triumphs. In 1977, his ex-wife Susan Glassman sued him for a share of the $160,000 Nobel Prize cash award as part of her alimony settlement. The courts ruled in her favor, but Bellow, considering the ruling unjust, refused to pay. He was sentenced to ten days in jail for contempt of court, and was ready to serve his time rather than surrender any more money to Glassman. After two years of appeals, countercharges, and bitter negotiations, the Illinois Appelate Court reversed the 1977 sentencing, but required Bellow to pay back alimony to the tune of some $500,000, plus $800 a month in child support.

After publishing *To Jerusalem and Back* (1976), a compelling pro-Israeli account/personal memoir of an extended visit to the Holy Land, Bellow returned to short fiction and journalism for the next few years, appearing now and then in the pages of *The New Yorker, The Atlantic Monthly,* and *Newsday,* as well as in lecture halls here and abroad, most notably at Oxford University. By 1980, he began spending most of his time in the foothills of southern Vermont, where he retreated to escape the unexpected and unwelcome onslaught of media attention and academic "suprecertification."

Despite his temporary withdrawal from the public eye, Bellow had no intention of being forgotton, or worse, cast in bronze. "The worst fear I have as a writer is that of losing my feeling for the common life," he told *The New York Times Book Review* the year he won the Nobel Prize. "To think of oneself as a Nobel Prize winner is finally to think of oneself as an enameled figurine in a China cabinet and I don't intend to find myself in a China cabinet."

Bellow emerged from the China cabinet in 1982 with what he referred to as a *cri de coeur* (cry of the heart)— a cry which he wasn't sure "anyone heard"—*The Dean's December*. The book was generally panned by the critics and is certainly one of his darkest novels, focusing as it does on death and the decline of urban living.

In 1984, Bellow the village storyteller returned in *Him With His Foot in His Mouth and Other Stories*, a collection of new and previously published material, including the novella *What Kind of Day Did You Have?* With their focus on family, tragicomic relationships, charlatans and victims, old-time Chicago, and self-awakenings, the stories hearken back to the old familiar Bellow of the Augie March/Moses Herzog days. The book remains a favorite among critics and readers alike.

The same Humboldt–Augie Marchian "mix of cerebration and antic plotting," as Kiernan put it, permeated Bellow's next novel, *More Die of Heartbreak* (1987). The story concerns the touching relationship between two eccentrics—middle-aged Russian literature professor Kenneth Trachtenberg and his globe-trotting botanist uncle Benn Crader—both engaged in a chaotic pursuit of happiness through the booby-trapped jungle of modern sexual politics and romance.

In his more recent novels, Bellow has continued to explore, to question, what it means to be a member of American society today, with its various pressures; what it means to be Jewish in a cultural melting pot, whether one is a Jew first and citizen second, or vice versa. In *A Theft* (1989), Bellow continues a long-standing quarrel with psychiatry and those who pretend to have insight into human nature. Protagonist Ithiel Regler tells heroine Clara Velde not to expect much from her psychiatrist, having been through enough therapy himself to know better. "If a millipede came into the office, he'd leave with an infinitesimal crutch for each leg," he declares. In the novella *The Bellarosa Connection* (1989), the unnamed Jewish-American narrator searches for his cultural roots in the richly drawn figures from the past, Harry Fonstein, war veteran and former POW (prisoner of war), the Yiddish actress Mrs. Hamet, and Broadway legend Billy Rose (the "Bellarosa" of the title). They are gone now, and so are the narrator's clearly defined claims to his Jewishness, leaving him feeling "like a socket that remembers its tooth." *A Theft* and *The Bellarosa Connection* were republished in 1991, together with the title story in the collection *Something to Remember Me By*.

Saul Bellow is without question one of our greatest living novelists, and ranks among the best American writers of all time. "His private investigations of reality," as biographer and friend Ruth Miller put it, "himself as individual, himself as member, himself as citizen, himself as artist fabricating conflicts between intellect and passion, reason and sexuality, ideals and hoax, are his long letter to us." Like Humboldt, the main character in *Humboldt's Gift*, he is an old-world figure, classically trained in the Proustian literary tradition of rich language and poetic insights, yet who, unlike his tragic hero, is a survivor who hasn't so much changed with the times as he has kept a close eye on them. And, in the final analysis, he has, in his long career, detected more hope for humanity than despair.

Chronology

June 10, 1915	born Solomon Bellow, in Quebec, Canada
1924	family moves to Chicago
1933-37	enrolls at University of Chicago; later transfers to Northwestern University, graduates class of '37 with an honors degree in sociology and anthropology; accepts scholarship to the University of Wisconsin to work on master's degree in anthropology, but drops out in mid-term and returns to Chicago; marries Anita Goshkin
1938–42	teaches at Pestalozzi-Froebel Teachers' College in Chicago; first son, Gregory, born; publishes first short story, "Two Morning Monologues" (1941); befriends poet and critic, Delmore Schwartz
1944	first novel, *The Dangling Man*
1948–50	in Paris on a Guggenheim Fellowship
1953	*The Adventures of Augie March*
1956	divorces Anita, marries Alexandra Tachacbasoz; moves to Tivoli, New York to teach at Bard College; *Seize the Day*
1959	*Henderson the Rain King*
1960	divorces Alexandra, marries Susan Glassman a year later

1964   *Herzog*

1967   travels to Middle East to cover
          Six-Day War for *Newsday*

1968   divorces Susan; *Mosby's Memoirs
          and Other Stories*

1970   *Mr. Sammler's Planet*

1975   marries Alexandra Ionescu Tulcea;
          Humboldt's Gift

1976   wins Pulitzer Prize for *Humboldt's
          Gift;* wins Nobel Prize for
          Literature; *To Jerusalem and Back*

1977   is sued by ex-wife Susan Glassman
          for a share of the Nobel Prize cash
          award; refuses to pay and is
          sentenced to ten days in jail; two
          years later Illinois Appelate Court
          reverses the 1977 sentencing, but
          requires Bellow to pay back
          alimony and child support

1980   moves to Vermont on
          semipermanent basis

1982   *The Dean's December*

1987   *More Die of Heartbreak*

1991   *Something to Remember Me By*,
          includes previously published
          novellas *A Theft* and *The Bellarosa
          Connection* (both 1989)

Further Reading

Bellow's Works

The Adventures of Augie March (New York: Viking Press, 1953). The rambling, picaresque novel that launched Bellow's career.

Seize the Day and Other Stories (New York: Viking Press, 1956). Bellow's arresting novella about a man who loses and regains his soul.

Herzog (New York: Viking Press, 1964). A tragicomic exploration of intellect, marriage, and the search for self.

Humboldt's Gift (New York: Viking Press, 1975). Bellow's Pulitzer Prize–winning look at the death of literature in modern society.

To Jerusalem and Back (New York: Viking, 1976). Popular and moving memoir of an American Jew's connection to Isreal, in the context of world politics.

It All Adds Up: From the Dim Past to the Uncertain Future (New York: Viking Press, 1994). A nonfiction collection, including two insightful interviews with the author.

Books About Bellow

Malcolm Bradbury, *Saul Bellow* (New York: Methuen Inc., 1982). Concise, comprehensive critical study of the major works, up to and including *The Dean's December*. Part of Methuen's Contemporary Writers series.

Ruth Miller, *Saul Bellow, A Biography of the Imagination* (New York: St. Martin's Press, 1991). Personal and critical examination of the life and works of Saul Bellow. Includes exhaustive bibliography of major works, the short stories, essays, and speeches, plus interviews with and profiles of Bellow. An excellent resource.

Robert F. Kiernan, *Saul Bellow* (New York: The Continuum Publishing Company, 1989). Thorough study of the major works, up to and including *More Die of Heatbreak*. Also contains biographical chapter, plus a bibliography.

J. D. Salinger
(1919–   )

*Rare publicity photograph of reclusive author
J. D. Salinger, taken around the time of the
publication of his classic* The Catcher in the Rye.
*Salinger's last published story appeared in 1964.
He has since steadfastly refused to publish
another word, although he has assured friends he
is still writing.*
(National Archives)

*I*n the fall of 1953, Shirlie Blaney, a sixteen-year-old high-school student from Windsor, Vermont, made "journalistic history" (as *Life* magazine's Ernest Havemann put it). Her scoop? An exclusive interview with J. D. Salinger, one of the most popular yet mysterious and reclusive figures in American literary history.

Blaney and some of her classmates were in desperate need of a story to fill the high-school page of their local paper, the Claremont *Daily Eagle,* when they noticed Salinger walking along Main Street in downtown Windsor. The famous author, who had recently moved to a secluded hillside home in nearby Cornish, New Hampshire, fiercely guarded his privacy, but always had time for the local students, whose company he seemed to greatly enjoy.

"He was just like one of the gang," Blaney later told *Life.* "I never saw anyone fit in the way he did."

And so Salinger said "Sure," when Blaney asked him for an interview. While she and her friends sipped Cokes in a booth at Harrington's Spa, Salinger sat across from them eating a sandwich and shared some of the rarely disclosed facts of his life, among them that his best-selling (and only) novel, *The Catcher in the Rye* (1951), was autobiographical.

"My boyhood was very much the same as that of the boy in the book," he told Blaney, referring to troubled teenage protagonist Holden Caulfield. "[I]t was a great relief telling people about it."

Realizing that Blaney had staged a major coup, the *Eagle* editor, to Salinger's shock, ran the interview prominently on the op-ed page. Soon after, a forbidding fence went up around the author's house and his friendship with the students was over.

Outside of a few other public statements here and there, Salinger has remained silent and aloof over the years. He spurns all inquiries, declines any comment whatsoever. He refuses even to publish anymore, which he similarly considers an invasion of his privacy, although he has assured friends that he is still writing. His entire body of (published) work consists of the one novel, a collection of nine short stories, two books of medium- and novella-length short fiction, plus a handful of early uncollected stories that appeared in magazines and journals primarily during the forties. Still, Salinger's books remain popular, both on bookstore shelves and in the classroom. Worldwide sales of *The Catcher in the Rye* alone approach a quarter of a million copies annually and the book has been a cult favorite on college and high school campuses for decades.

Despite the fact that Salinger prefers to let his characters and their stories speak exclusively for him, ("Read the book[s]. It's all there in the book[s]," he insisted to one interviewer who ambushed him in Windsor), some facts of his life are available, although they are minimal at best and sketchy at worst. A handful of magazine articles, newspaper reports and the introductions to a few critical works are about all that most recent biographers have had to work with ever since Salinger retreated to the New Hampshire hills in 1953. Even these accounts are not always reliable, as Salinger has been known to leave false clues here and there.

The record does tell us that Jerome David Salinger was born on January 1, 1919, in New York City, the second and last child of Sol and Mirriam Jillich Salinger. Salinger's father, a Jew, was an importer of hams and cheeses and, according to some sources, the son of a rabbi. His mother was a Scotch-Irish gentile who changed her name from Marie to Mirriam, so as to better fit into the Salinger family. We know little of Salinger's sister, Doris, other than that she was eight years older than Sonny, as Salinger was called in his youth, and that she eventually became a buyer at Bloomingdale's.

After attending public grade school, Salinger was enrolled in 1932 at Manhattan's McBurney School, an expensive private institution, where, like Holden, he did poorly in most of his classes and was manager of the fencing team. His school records state his only interests were journalism, drama, and tropical fish. A childhood friend recalled that Salinger was a distant adolescent, "the kind of kid who, if you wanted to have a card game, wouldn't join in."

Concerned about Sonny's behavior and grades, Sol Salinger sent his boy off to Valley Forge Military Academy, "a seat of heavy learning, fortified with boxwood hedges and Revolutionary War cannon . . . in the Pennsylvania Hills" as *Time* magazine's Jack Skow described it.

J. D. Salinger

*The Valley Forge Military Academy in Pennsylvania, where Salinger was a
student during the thirties, served as the model for* The Catcher in the
Rye's *Pencey Prep. Many of Salinger's classmates and teachers inspired
characters in the book*
(Courtesy Valley Forge Military Academy and College)

Valley Forge was almost certainly the inspiration for
Catcher's Pencey Prep. The school's mission (as quoted in Ian
Hamilton's 1988 biography, *In Search of J. D. Salinger*) was to
turn out "young men . . . alert in mind, sound in body, consid-
erate of others, and with a high sense of duty, honor, loyalty
and courage." Pencey Prep's motto boasted of "molding boys
into splendid, clear-thinking young men," a claim that Holden
considers "strictly for the birds." It was at Valley Forge that
Salinger met the snobs and the bullies, the jocks and the
pompous school administrators who served as models for
Catcher's Ackley, Stradlater, Marsalla, and old Headmaster
Thurmer.

Yet Salinger found some satisfaction in several extracurricular activities at Valley Forge: he joined the dramatics club and was literary editor of the yearbook. It was also during these years that Salinger seriously began to consider becoming a writer. His earliest short stories (now lost) were written by flashlight under cover of a blanket after "lights out" in the dormitory.

Sol Salinger, however, was skeptical of his son's career plans. After a brief spell at New York University upon graduation from Valley Forge in 1936, Sonny was shipped off to Europe the following year to improve his foreign-language skills (French and German) and learn the import-export business.

Returning to New York in the spring of 1938 convinced that his father's line of work was not for him, Salinger thought he'd give higher education another try and enrolled at Ursinus College, a small liberal arts institution in Collegeville, Pennsylvania. He quickly tired of academic life, however, with its tests and lectures. He was equally bored socially, his sophisticated New York wit and manners earning him a reputation as a loner among his middle-class suburban classmates. He left Ursinus after one semester with little to show for his efforts save for a handful of snide columns and reviews that he penned for the campus newspaper.[*]

The first significant turning point in Salinger's career came in 1939 when he enrolled in a famous short-story class at Columbia University taught by Whit Burnett. Burnett was editor of *Story* magazine and the first publisher of such rising stars as Norman Mailer, Truman Capote, Tennessee Williams, and others. At the time, the short story was a popular and highly marketable form of entertainment and *Story* was but one of dozens of magazines of the day publishing short fiction.

Setting his sights on *The New Yorker,* the most sophisticated and prestigious of the pack, Salinger, at twenty, was now fully committed to a life of serious creative writing. Burnett's wife,

---

[*]Salinger's lack of a diploma would remain a sore point. He once turned on a couple of shocked party guests when the conversation shifted to where they had all gone to college. Enraged, he called them leeches and parasites and castigated them for over two hours before they finally left.

Hallie (coauthor with her husband of *Fiction Writer's Handbook*), recalls the aloof and brooding young author during those first few weeks at Columbia:

> [T]here was one dark-eyed, thoughtful young man who sat through one semester of class in writing without taking notes, seemingly not listening, looking out the window. A week or so before the semester ended, he suddenly came to life. He began to write. Several stories seemed to come from his typewriter at once and most of these were [eventually] published. That young man was J. D. Salinger . . .

Whit Burnett, recognizing talent and potential, accepted one of Salinger's classroom pieces for *Story*. This first published Salinger short story, "The Young Folks" (1940), concerned a socially awkward young man, Bill Jameson, falsely accused of propositioning a snobbish, adolescent girl at a party.

Neatly crafted (Whit Burnett, as quoted by Hamilton, observed that Salinger "was the kind [of writer] who ingests and then comes out with very edited material"), "The Young Folks" is noted for introducing a classic Salinger theme, that of the young innocent confronting what critic Dan Wakefield has termed "the deadening rituals of pretense" among the "phonies" of the adult world.

Salinger followed up "The Young Folks" that year with "Go See Eddie" in the *University of Kansas City Review*, an academic "little" magazine, which added a touch of credibility to the reputation he was gradually building for himself. Never losing sight of his literary Holy Grail—*The New Yorker*—he came to the cold realization that he would have to compromise his artistic integrity and churn out some of the formulaic stuff popular with editors of the so-called "slick" magazines like *The Saturday Evening Post*. "The Hang of It" (1941), an army story written to length and with a cutesy twist of an ending, was such a work and it got him into the pages of *Collier's*, the break he needed. Later that year he sold a more sophisticated piece, "The Heart of a Broken Story" to *Esquire*.

Though some are trivial, these early stories display many of the stylistic and thematic elements for which Salinger would become famous. They focus on personal relationships, particularly among families, and as critic Arthur Mizener notes "[t]hey make clear [Salinger's] marked preference for first-person narrative and interior monologue."

Another of Salinger's trademarks is his masterful ear for dialect, which has been frequently compared to that of an earlier, great American stylist, Ring Lardner. By emphasizing words or syllables in italics and spelling them idiomatically—"Wudga say?", "How *marv*elous," "It's a terrific bore," "What the hellja do *that* for?", "You in chahge heah, Sahgeant?", "I was asleep, for Crissake"—Salinger captures the vernacular of a broad range of characters with stunning accuracy, from pretentious Upper East Side debutantes to gruff, wisecracking cab drivers. Similarly his gift for smooth, natural-sounding dialogue has been widely praised by critics.

An acceptance letter from *The New Yorker* finally arrived in 1941 for "Slight Rebellion off Madison," Salinger's first story of a troubled youth named Holden Caulfield who wants to run away from prep school. This triumph was a brief one, however. The editors decided to delay the story's publication: it was their view that stories about runaways were contrary to the patriotic spirit of America's recent entry into World War II.

Salinger himself entered the war the following year when he was drafted into the army. He served in both the Signal and Counter Intelligence Corps and was among the expeditionary forces storming the beaches of Normandy on D day. In his spare moments from 1942 to 1945, when he was discharged, he worked on and off at his Holden Caulfield story (the genesis of *The Catcher in the Rye*) while still producing material for popular magazines.

The degree to which the second world war impacted Salinger's life and fiction is open to debate. Some critics consider the war as *the* defining experience of Salinger's literary career. James Lundquist has written: "Salinger should be read as a writer who is seeking solutions, as a writer who is trying to give direction to his thought based on an initial disturbing event. And that event is World War II."

There is some evidence, writes biographer Ian Hamilton, that Salinger suffered a nervous breakdown during this time. We also learn that while in Europe he suddenly married a French doctor. Little is known about the woman other than that her first name was Sylvia and that she may have been a psychologist (some say psychiatrist or osteopath). According to evidence unearthed by Hamilton, the marriage lasted only eight months. After returning to the States with his bride in May of 1946, Salinger allegedly announced in Florida that he was divorced and that his former wife had returned to Europe.*

Like so many other returned veterans in the postwar years of 1946–47, Salinger stood poised on the edge of an uncertain yet potentially promising future. There had been some discussion with Whitt Burnett about the possibility of a short-story collection; Simon and Schuster had courted him with a similar proposal, but he told them he wanted to wait. It was around this time, according to Hamilton, that "Salinger as a man of mystery might be said to have made his first appearance": on the contributor's notes page of a 1947 issue of *Mademoiselle* magazine Salinger declares that he "does not believe in contributors' columns" and will only divulge that he has been writing since he was eight, was in the army, and "almost always writes of young people."

In December of 1945, "I'm Crazy"—the story of Holden Caulfield's dismissal from prep school—appeared in *Collier's*. It was Salinger's first published work to include material that would later be used in *The Catcher in the Rye*. A year later, *The New Yorker* finally published the other Holden story, "Slight Rebellion off Madison," that it had been sitting on since

---

*As with many details of Salinger's life, this one remains a convoluted mystery. *Life* magazine claimed "it is definitely established that Salinger married a woman whom he met while serving overseas . . . and divorced her in Florida in 1947 . . ." while Salinger biographer Warren French says there is no evidence in Florida state records that proves that Salinger was granted a divorce in that year. Meanwhile, Ian Hamilton asserts that "Sylvia" went back to France to get her divorce and Salinger himself has denied that there ever was such a marriage!

1941.[*] In 1946, Salinger submitted but then withdrew a ninety page novella concerning Holden which had been accepted by a publisher (we don't know which one). Though simmering, *The Catcher in the Rye* hadn't yet reached a full boil; in fact at this point Salinger didn't believe that he'd ever write a novel: "I'm a dash man not a miler," he had told *Esquire* magazine.

His long-awaited badge of literary honor came at a fairly cold and unproductive time in his life. Home from the war with no immediate plans, he was living with his parents and spent much of his time playing poker, frequenting Greenwich Village blues clubs, and grumbling about the "editorial manhandling" he was forced to endure in the popular magazines. He was furious after the titles of a couple of his stories in *The Saturday Evening Post* had been changed ("Both Parties Concerned" and "Soft-Boiled Sergeant" had originally been titled "Wake Me When It Thunders" and "Death of a Dogface") and vowed to never again allow such violations.

He wouldn't have to. With the publication of "A Perfect Day for Bananafish" in 1948, Salinger commenced what would become an almost exclusive relationship with *The New Yorker*. A string of acceptances followed, among them some of Salinger's most famous and impressive stories such as "Uncle Wiggily in Connecticut" (1948), "Just before the War with the Eskimos" (1948), and "For Esmé—with Love and Squalor" (1950).

"Bananafish" is one of Salinger's most unusual, troubling, and analyzed stories. It also marks the first appearance of one of his most psychologically complex characters, Seymour Glass, the "near saint" and "family guru," as *Time*'s Jack Scow

---

*Although the Holden Caulfields in these and earlier stories share many of the same experiences, it is impossible to piece together an accurate chronological biography of *The Catcher in the Rye*'s Holden by examining them altogether. Holden could not, as Warren French has observed, for instance, presumably die in combat during World War II, in the early short story, "This Sandwich Has No Mayonnaise," and then show up as an adolescent in *Catcher* mentioning incidents that occurred in 1949; *Catcher* cultists may also be delighted to find that in "I'm Crazy," Holden has a baby sister, Viola, who is younger than Phoebe, and learn in "Slight Rebellion off Madison" that his middle name is Morrisey—details that do not appear in the novel.

wrote, who would remain a central figure in much of the rest of Salinger's fiction.

Salinger's stories such as "A Perfect Day for Bananafish" are often unsettling and enigmatic. Like the details of his private life, the author appears to be purposefully withholding information from the reader. This attitude might seem peevish, but it could offer insight into why he eventually became a recluse with no further interest in publishing, to the dismay and disappointment of his reading public.

If Salinger's characters "have a real life that extends beyond a story's dramatic confines," i.e., in his imagination, the creative act of simply writing, in and of itself, was enough for him. He was no longer writing for an audience, he was beginning to write for himself.

His literary arrival in the pages of *The New Yorker* made him a subject of conversation among the smart New York literary and intellectual circles—a crowd whose attention he apparently craved but whose company he seemed to despise.

As the title character of the story "Franny" (1955) muses: "I know when they're going to be so *charming*, I know when they're going to start telling you some really nasty gossip . . . and start bragging in a terribly, terribly quiet voice—or *name-dropping* . . . There's an unwritten law that people in a certain social or financial bracket can name-drop as much as they like just as long as they say something terribly disparaging about the person as soon as they've dropped his name . . ."

Salinger attempted to escape this scene by moving to Westport, Connecticut, where, as he told *The Saturday Review,* he "lived alone, with a big American dog and a little English car." It was during this time, from 1948 to 1950, that he apparently resumed work on his Holden Caulfield novel. His writing schedule was "spasmodic"; sometimes he would put in 16- to 18-hour days, then stay away from his desk for weeks.

Salinger's series of *New Yorker* successes had piqued the interest of several publishers—among them Robert Giroux, then at Harcourt Brace—eager to know if he was writing a novel and offering to publish his short stories. As recounted in

Hamilton, Salinger failed to reply to a letter from Giroux but months later showed up in the publisher's office saying, "It's not my stories that should be published first, but the novel I'm working on . . . about this kid in New York during the Christmas holidays . . ." They shook hands on the deal and Salinger worked feverishly to complete the book, dividing his time between Westport and a hot, steamy room near the Third Avenue El.

When Salinger finally delivered the manuscript, Giroux (as quoted in Hamilton) "thought it a remarkable book" and considered himself "lucky to be its editor." Giroux's luck would be short-lived, however. As scholar Henry Anatole Grunwald recounts, the deal began to sour when Harcourt Brace asked for a rewrite. Salinger immediately contacted his agent to have him get the manuscript back. When asked to explain, he said that he could not possibly work with his editor.

"Why," fumed Salinger, "the man thought Holden was crazy."

The book ended up in the hands of Boston's Little, Brown where more sparks flew when the firm tried to drum up a little prepublication publicity. Salinger resisted every effort: no press, no review copies, not even a picture on the dust jacket (an author photo did appear on the first two editions, but Salinger had it yanked off by the third).

The Catcher in the Rye remains one of the most popular and, some believe, important and influential novels of late twentieth-century American literature. It has been called everything from an "anthem" to "obscene" to a "manifesto against the world" for "generation[s] of high school and college students," many of whom could probably recite the book's famous opening lines more readily than they could the preamble to the Constitution:

> *If you really want to hear about it, the first thing you'll probably want to know is where I was born, and what my lousy childhood was like, and how my parents were occupied and all before they had me, and all that David Copperfield kind of crap, but I don't feel like going into it, if you want to know the truth.*

With this ambivalent invitation, Holden takes us along on his three-day journey of self-discovery and spiritual growth on the streets of New York City.

The Catcher in the Rye is more than just the story of a tortured adolescent struggling with growing up, although it clearly succeeds as such. As critics Arthur Heiserman and James E. Miller, Jr. have observed, *Catcher* belongs to an "ancient and honorable narrative tradition" in Western literature as old as Homer's *Odyssey*, i.e., the "Quest," the search for truth by an heroic character who is typically at odds with his environment.

Holden appears to be such a hero. Surrounded by "phonies" and hypocrites, he longs to escape the shallow pettiness and corruption of the adult world, a world inhabited by "[g]uys that always talk about how many miles they get to a gallon in their goddam cars [and] . . . get sore and childish as hell if you beat them at golf, or even just some stupid game like ping-pong."

Holden's sense of justice and fair-play, his frank readiness, internally at least, to cut through "the old bull" and pretensions of society are among his most endearing and amusing qualities. He tells us that Pencey's advertisements always feature "some hot-shot guy on a horse jumping over a fence" when in fact he "never even once saw a horse anywhere near the place." He hates "always saying 'Glad to've met you' to somebody I'm not at *all* glad I met." He is fed up with "[t]axicabs and Madison Avenue buses . . . and going up and down in elevators when you just want to go outside, and guys fitting your pants all the time at Brooks . . ." It is always the "hot-shots" who are winning the "game" of life in Holden's world.

Holden's caustic remarks, wisecracks, and vernacular, wrote critic Alfred Kazin, have made him "a favorite" with students and young people "who respond to him with a consciousness that he speaks for them and virtually *to* them, in a language that is peculiarly honest and their own, with a vision . . . that captures their most secret judgments of the world."

Through the course of the book, the reader may realize that it is not *truth* that Holden seeks so much as stability. He is comforted by life's various constants, like the Indian room at the Museum of Natural History ("The best thing . . . in that museum was that everything always stayed right where it was.") or the feel of a skate key in his hand. Children, so reliable in their behavior and attitudes, so virtuous and innocent, provide the most stability Holden has ever known. It is his one ambition, he tells his kid sister Phoebe, to preserve this innocence forever:

> *I keep picturing all these little kids playing some game in this big field of rye and all. Thousands of little kids, and nobody's around—nobody big, I mean—except me. And I'm standing on the edge of some crazy cliff. What I have to do, I have to catch everybody if they start to go over the cliff—I mean if they're running and they don't look where they're going I have to come out from somewhere and catch them. That's all I'd do all day. I'd just be the catcher in the rye . . .*

The edge of Holden's "crazy cliff" is the threshold of adulthood and a principal source of his frustration is his inability to remain perched there. He *must* grow up and what pushes him over the edge, says scholar James Lundquist, is "his realization of the essential obscenity of life itself" as symbolized by the four-letter words he finds etched on the walls of Phoebe's school and defiling the sanctity of the museum.

"You can't ever find a place that's nice and peaceful," he declares, "because there isn't any."

Critical reactions to *Catcher* were mixed. *The New Yorker*, naturally, had nothing but kind words for their author, and *The New York Times* called the book an "unusually brilliant first novel." The magazines were less impressed. *The Nation* sneered that *Catcher* "was not at all something rich and strange, but what every sensitive 16-year old since Rousseau has felt," while *Commentary* magazine seized the opportunity to attack not only *Catcher* but the whole *New Yorker* school of fiction. Predictably, the Christian publications, such as *Catholic World*, expressed profound shock at Holden's language and the *Christian Science Monitor* feared that the book's "immorality and perversion" would corrupt innocent teen-aged minds.[*]

Nevertheless, *Catcher* remained on *The New York Times* best-seller list for close to a year and steadily gained popularity among undergraduates. "Salinger's name came to dominate dormitory bull sessions and to be spoken of in the worshipful tones once reserved for Hemingway," according to scholar Sanford Pinsker in his study of the novel. This reverence eventually attracted the attention of scholars who "came to scoff [but] stayed to pray."

Like it or not, Salinger was now a public figure. In 1951, he left Westport and returned to Manhattan, where he hoped he could just disappear.

"I feel tremendously relieved that the season for success of *The Catcher in the Rye* is over," he told *The Saturday Review* the following year. "I enjoyed a small part of it, but most of it I found . . . professionally and personally demoralizing."

It was around this time that Salinger became increasingly interested in the study of Eastern religions, especially Zen Buddhism and the teachings of Sri Ramakrishna, a nineteenth-century Hindu mystic who preached acceptance of all religions. Eastern philosophy emphasized the universality of the human spirit and its inherent connection to God plus a belief in reincarnation; spiritual enlightenment was the ultimate reward for a life dedicated to intense meditation, yoga, and the constant contemplation of the Absolute.

Other writers of the "Beat Generation," such as Jack Kerouac and Allen Ginsberg, plus influential rock bands like The Beatles would later popularize Eastern religions during the fifties and sixties, making them faddish among rebellious young Western-ers; it is worth noting, however, that Salinger was one of the first major American artists of his generation to turn to these philosophies and integrate them into his work.

---

[*]To this day, *The Catcher in the Rye* remains banned from many school and public libraries. Salinger once wrote that because all of his "best friends are children . . . [i]t's almost unbearable . . . to realize that my book will be kept on a shelf out of their reach."

In Salinger's next published book, a short story collection simply titled *Nine Stories,* he explores a central theme. The unifying thread can be found in the Zen riddle, or koan, with which Salinger introduces the book:

We know the sound of two hands clapping.
But what is the sound of one hand clapping?

Like a Zen master, Salinger is suggesting that "the sound of one hand clapping" is something to ponder; that the answer to the question will not be arrived at easily or quickly, as in the process of reincarnation the soul must progress through many lives before obtaining perfection. "Revealing his preoccupation with human beings living in the aftermath of some fall from a once saving grace," wrote critic John Wenke in his study of Salinger's short fiction, "Salinger presents in *every* story some version of a lost idyll, lost innocence, lost past, or lost opportunity." Just as the riddle of the koan requires creative thought and insight, redemption is available only for those characters in *Nine Stories* who have epiphanies, momentary glimpses of truth, and are thus equipped to "remain spiritually *nice* in a *phony* world," as scholar Warren French put it.

In January of 1953, on his birthday, Salinger left New York for good and moved to the rural town of Cornish, New Hampshire. Although he shared Holden's desire for a quiet life, Salinger wasn't exactly a hermit. He gave cocktail parties for neighbors, puzzled more than a few, no doubt, with yoga demonstrations, and, as we have seen, enjoyed entertaining local young people. In February of 1955, he married Claire Douglas, a British-born, nineteen-year-old Radcliffe student who gave birth later that year to their first child, Margaret Ann; a son, Mathew, was born five years later.

Salinger built a cinder-block work studio on the property, with a translucent plastic roof for light. Neighbors said he would amble down the hill to his studio at 5 or 6 A.M. and put in fifteen or sixteen hours of work, chain-smoking the whole time. He kept sheaves of notes on various plots and characters clipped to cup hooks along the wall, taking down a clip and making notations whenever an idea occurred to him. He was now exclusively focusing his efforts on what he called a long-term project, "a narrative series . . . about a family of settlers in twentieth-century New York, the Glasses."

Salinger published a total of five Glass family stories, although he assured readers in 1963 that he had "several new" ones "coming along," which in fact will probably never appear in his lifetime given his stated aversion to publishing. These five stories, all of which had their debuts in *The New Yorker*, are, in order of publication: "Franny," "Raise High the Roof Beam, Carpenters" (1955), "Zooey" (1957), "Seymour—an Introduction" (1959), and "Hapworth 16, 1924" (1965), which remains Salinger's last published story to date. *Franny and Zooey* appeared as a collection in 1961 followed by *Raise High the Roof Beam, Carpenters and Seymour—an Introduction* two years later.

Franny and Zooey takes aim at the smug and trendy Ivy League crowd of pseudo-intellectuals while examining the destructive effects such trends have had on the two youngest Glass family members of the title. *Raise High the Roof Beam, Carpenters and Seymour—an Introduction* and "Hapworth 16, 1924" continue to explore the mind and motivation of Seymour Glass, as told by Buddy in "Raise High" and the "Introduction," and by Seymour himself as a teenager writing home from summer camp in "Hapworth." Salinger's plots and prose become increasingly enigmatic in these stories as he reaches deeper and deeper into Seymour's/his own psyche. Only the most devoted readers were (and have been) able to follow him here and the critics were becoming less patient with his self-indulgence as well.

"Salinger loves the Glasses more than God loves them," John Updike complained in *The New York Times Book Review*. "He loves them too exclusively. Their invention has become a hermitage for him. He loves them to the detriment of artistic moderation."

In a *Nation* article entitled "The Salinger Industry," critic George Steiner wrote that "[Salinger] demands of his readers nothing in the way of literacy or political interest." He goes on to lament the "serious devaluation" of literary criticism when lavished too generously on Salinger whom he calls "interesting" and certainly worthy of discussion and praise, but "not in terms appropriate to the master poets of the world." Mary McCarthy, writing in *Harper's Magazine,* wonders just who all "these wonder kids"—the Glasses—are "but Salinger himself . . . To be confronted with the seven faces of Salinger . . . is to gaze into a terrifying narcissus pool. Salinger's world contains nothing but Salinger . . ."

None of this negative criticism, however, did much to diminish the sales of Salinger's books nor the public's curiosity about America's most mysterious man of letters. During the early sixties, New York editors from the major newsweeklies dispatched teams of journalists to scour the New Hampshire hills and return with a story on Salinger. They talked to old classmates, friends, neighbors, and store clerks. They staked out his driveway, the post office, and the grocery store hoping to ambush their subject. With a few exceptions, none got any closer to Salinger than the wooden fence surrounding the house. Those who did manage to approach him in person were given a cold stare followed by a quick and silent departure.

Salinger has resurfaced on several occasions since his retirement from public life. In 1974 he broke his silence to denounce the release of *The Complete Uncollected Short Stories of J. D. Salinger,* an unauthorized two-volume edition of his early, uncollected fiction published by a still-unidentified party in California. "[M]y property [has] been stolen," Salinger complained to a San Francisco–based *New York Times* reporter, the first journalist to speak on the record with the reclusive author since sixteen-year-old Shirlie Blaney interviewed him for the Claremont *Daily Eagle* in 1953. Salinger later won his suit against several San Francisco booksellers for distributing the pirated collection. In 1981, *The Catcher in the Rye* made headlines once more when Mark David Chapman, deranged assassin of former Beatle John Lennon, claimed that his crime was influenced by the novel and that he identified himself with Holden Caulfield.* Salinger took legal action to protect his privacy once more in 1986 and won an injunction against the publication of an unauthorized biography by British writer Ian Hamilton. Hamilton had paraphrased and used excerpts from many of Salinger's unpublished letters, documents which Salinger claimed were his copyrighted property. A revised version of Hamilton's *In Search of J. D. Salinger,* stripped of its quotes from and rephrasing of Salinger's correspondence, was published in 1988.

One explanation for Salinger's enduring popularity—among critics, educators, and the reading public in general—is that, like F. Scott Fitzgerald, he brilliantly captured the spirit of a generation, a population of postwar adolescents who had serious moral doubts concerning the adult world they were about to enter.

"I almost always write about very young people," Salinger once noted, and indeed one of the attractive ironies of Salinger's fictive world is that it is children, not adults, who are the insightful ones, the visionaries, the poets. Of these troubled, young protagonists, Holden Caulfield remains Salinger's most famous and, as scholar Sanford Pinsker notes, has joined the roster of such great American characters as Melville's Bartleby, Hawthorne's Young Goodman Brown, Twain's Huck Finn, James' Daisy Miller, Fitzgerald's Daisy Buchanan, and Hemingway's Nick Adams.

As a stylist, Salinger comes closest to Twain for his masterful use of vernacular, in addition to his critical views of conventional society. While his earlier (and arguably most popular) work is more traditional—similar in quality to Updike or O'Connor—Salinger's later (published) material is most like that of Vonnegut or Kerouac in that it challenges tradition and form. So, even though he has not published anything in over thirty years, J. D. Salinger continues to be a part of an ongoing movement in American letters—a movement to cast aside the old molds and discover new modes of artistic expression.

---

*When police arrived at the scene of the shooting, they found Chapman waiting there, calmly reading *Catcher*.

Chronology

January 1, 1919	born in New York City
1932–36	attends exclusive McBurney School in Manhattan; transfers to and graduates from Valley Forge Military Academy in Pennsylvania, class of '36
1936–38	to Europe, at behest of father, for two-year apprenticeship in import-export business; expresses little interest in the profession; returns to the States and enrolls at Ursinus College in Pennsylvania; enjoys writing column for campus publication, but is otherwise bored and drops out after a semester
1939–40	enrolls in short-story class at Columbia University taught by Whitt Burnett, editor of *Story* magazine; first story, "The Young Folks" (1940) published in *Story*; "Go See Eddie" also published in the *University of Kansas City Review*
1941	"Slight Rebellion off Madison," the first story to mention Holden Caulfield, is accepted by *The New Yorker* but magazine delays publication until 1946
1942–45	is drafted into the army, serves in Europe during World War II and is at Normandy on D Day; works on "Holden" novel in spare time; "I'm

Crazy," first published work to include material later used in *The Catcher in the Rye,* appears in *Collier's* (1945); allegedly marries, and later divorces, a mysterious French doctor named "Sylvia"

1948 "A Perfect Day for Bananafish" appears in *The New Yorker*; marks beginning of long string of acceptances by the magazine; moves to Westport, Connecticut, and works on *Catcher in the Rye*

1951 *The Catcher in the Rye*; leaves Westport and returns to New York; begins to study Zen Buddhism and the teachings of Sri Ramakrishna

1953 *Nine Stories*; seeks privacy by moving to Cornish, New Hampshire; gives interview to local student for the high-school page of local paper; is incensed when interview appears on op-ed page; vows to never speak to another reporter again

1955 marries Claire Douglas, British-born, nineteen-year-old Radcliffe student; first child, Margaret Ann, is born; a son, Mathew, is born five years later

1961 *Franny and Zooey*

1963 *Raise High the Roof Beam, Carpenters and Seymour—an Introduction*

1965 "Hapworth 16, 1924," last published story to date, appears in *The New Yorker*

1967 divorces Claire

1974 breaks longstanding silence to denounce *The Complete Uncollected Short Stories of J. D. Salinger,* an unauthorized two-volume edition of early, uncollected fiction

1986 in a landmark case, wins an injunction against the publication of an unauthorized biography by British writer Ian Hamilton, arguing that Hamilton had stolen copyrighted material by paraphrasing and using excerpts from unpublished letters; a revised version of Hamilton's *In Search of J. D. Salinger* is published in 1988

Further Reading

Salinger's Works

The Catcher in the Rye (Boston: Little, Brown and Co., 1951). The story of teenage anti-hero Holden Caulfield; Salinger's only published novel; a classic and a cult favorite among generations of young readers.

Nine Stories (Boston: Little, Brown and Co., 1953). Collection of many of Salinger's *New Yorker* stories.

Franny and Zooey (Boston: Little, Brown and Co., 1961). Two stories of Salinger's precious Glass family.

Raise High the Roof Beam, Carpenters and Seymour—An Introduction (Boston: Little, Brown and Co., 1963).

Books About Salinger

Harold Bloom, editor, *J. D. Salinger* (New York, New Haven, Philadelphia: Chelsea House Publishers, 1987). Collection of critical, scholarly essays; includes introduction by Bloom.

Warren French, *J. D. Salinger* (Boston: Twayne Publishers, 1963).

Warren French, *J. D. Salinger, Revisted* (Boston: Twayne Publishers, 1988). Authoratative, sympathetic critical biography by respected Salinger scholar; includes bibliography and chronology. Revised edition of earlier work.

Henry Anatole Grunwald, editor, *Salinger: A Critical and Personal Portrait* (New York: Harper, 1962). Excellent collection of critical, scholarly essays on all of Salinger's works. Introduction by Grunwald.

Ian Hamilton, *In Search of J. D. Salinger* (New York: Random House, 1988). Controversial biography of Salinger which inspired a landmark lawsuit; probably the most thorough biography to date; style is informal.

James Lundquist, *J. D. Salinger* (New York: Frederick Unger Publishing, Inc., 1979). Thorough, critical study, which analyzes Salinger's fiction in the context of Zen Buddhism.

Sanford Pinsker, *The Catcher in the Rye: Innocence Under Pressure* (New York: Twayne Publishers,1993). Comprehensive study of the novel, covering historical context, critical reception, and importance of the work; includes bibliography and chronology. Part of Twayne Masterworks Series.

John Wenke, *J. D. Salinger: A Study of the Short Fiction* (Boston: Twayne Publishers, 1991). Comprehensive study of the short stories, with excellent and concise biographical information, plus a chronology and bibliography.

Jack Kerouac
(1922–1969)

"Beat" author Jack Kerouac shattered literary traditions and inspired a generation of young people to take to the highways with his cult classic, On the Road.
(National Archives)

*I*n the spring of 1951, an enthusiastic young Jack Kerouac appeared in the office of Robert Giroux of Harcourt Brace bearing a huge, rumpled roll of paper. "Here's your novel!" declared the author as he let the roll—all 120 feet of it—unravel across the desk and office of the astonished editor. Kerouac had typed the 175,000-word, single-spaced, unparagraphed manuscript in one marathon three-week sitting. Realizing that the excited young writer was serious, Giroux sputtered, "But

Jack, how can you make corrections on a manuscript like that?" Kerouac indignantly claimed that he didn't make changes or corrections to his work, rolled up his novel, and stormed out the door.

The book, *On the Road* (1957), was eventually published by Viking and soon became the quintessential novel of the "Beat Generation," a literary and cultural movement rooted in New York's Greenwich Village jazz clubs of the fifties. By Kerouac's own definition, the Beats were a group of young men and women who "came of age after World War II" and sought escape from the disillusionment of the Cold War through "mystical detachment and relaxation of social and sexual tensions." They in turn contributed to the rise of the counterculture revolution of the sixties, one of the most socially turbulent decades in American history.

Kerouac became permanently identified as the spokesperson for the Beat Generation, living his own legend "on the road" with such cultural heroes as philosopher/drifter Neal Cassady, poet Allen Ginsberg, and contemporary Beat author William Burroughs. Kerouac modeled his rambling, free-form lyrical writing style—a style which he called "sketching" or "spontaneous prose"—on the rhythms of jazz music and the works of Marcel Proust and James Joyce. While he is most often spoken of as the chronicler of the Beat Generation (a label he would come to deny and resent), Kerouac's autobiographical writings, as scholar Ann Charters observed, "are among the most complete, dramatic, and devastating accounts in our country's literature of the high cost of acculturation paid by a sensitive and ambitious first-generation native son."

The third child of French-Canadian immigrants, Jack Kerouac (or Ti Jean, as he was called all his life by his mother) forever walked astride two cultures—French and American. Born in the factory town of Lowell, Massachusetts, on March 12, 1922, Jean Louis Lebris de Kerouac grew up in a close-knit community of fellow French-Canadians who shared a common tongue (*joual*, the Quebecois language), religion (Catholicism), and traditions. Joual was Kerouac's first language until he went to parochial school and he spoke it all his life with his mother Gabrielle, whom he affectionately called *mémère*.

Kerouac's earliest childhood memories were overshadowed by the lingering illness of his nine-year-old brother, Gerard, who eventually succumbed to rheumatic fever in July of 1926. The "poor sickly little Gerard," as his brother would recall him in *Visions of Gerard* (1963), became a martyr in Kerouac's fiction, a "religious hero" whose death, as Charters observed, posed "the philosophical riddle . . . why are we born but to die?"

Kerouac was 11 when he decided he was going to be a writer, scribbling "whole little novels in nickel notebooks" and idolizing Thomas Wolfe and adventure writer Jack London. An avid reader, he described in *Vanity of Duluoz* (1967)—one in a series of autobiographical novels—how he would "cut classes at least once a week" just "to go to the Lowell Public Library" where he could spend time "at leisure" in the company of Johann Wolfgang von Goethe, Victor Hugo, H. G. Wells, and other "such old things as chess books with their fragrance of scholarly thought."

An accomplished athlete, young Jack saw football as a way out of Lowell and by 1938 was being wooed by coaches at Boston College and Columbia University. He ultimately chose Columbia but before he could be accepted he needed to make up a few courses which he had failed at Lowell High. The Columbia coach helped arrange a football scholarship at the exclusive Horace Mann School for Boys in the Bronx—"a rich school for young Jews," as Kerouac later characterized it in *Maggie Cassidy* (1959). A poor, displaced factory-town kid, Kerouac made pocket money writing $2 term papers for wealthy classmates, some of whom would occasionally take pity on him in the cafeteria by sharing "a delicious fresh juicy chicken sandwich" after noticing his "humble awful lunch" (*Vanity*). One such lunchtime buddy introduced him to the writing of Ernest Hemingway. Kerouac admired the terse, manly style and tried to emulate it in his first published short story (appearing in the *Horace Mann*

Quarterly, "The Brothers," which, as biographer Tom Clark points out in *Jack Kerouac*, "owe[d] more to pulp detective style than Hemingway."

Kerouac left Horace Mann with few regrets in the spring of 1940, his visions of college life all laid out before him: "I, of all things, wanted to end up on campus somewhere smoking a pipe, with a buttondown sweater, like Bing Crosby serenading a coed in the moonlight . . . as the strains of alma mater song come from the frat house," he wrote in *Vanity*. His actual and somewhat short-lived experiences at Columbia were less conventional. He spent more time reading what he pleased rather than what he was assigned and hanging out in Times Square movie theaters instead of in the classroom. He eventually quit the football team and dropped out of school in the fall of his sophomore year.

Kerouac joined the navy soon after the bombing of Pearl Harbor on December 7, 1941, but, like college, his military career was a short one: unable to handle the discipline, he was given a psychiatric discharge after six months and shipped out for the North Atlantic in the merchant marine. When not at sea, he divided his time between his parents' new apartment on Long Island where he helped care for his ailing father, Leo, and New York City, where he became romantically involved with, and eventually married, art student Edie Parker. The marriage lasted only two months, but it was through Parker that Kerouac met a new crowd at Columbia—"the Bohemian kids from the neighborhood"—which included Ginsberg, Burroughs, and Lucien Carr.

These "city intellectuals," as Kerouac called them, read Rimbaud and Dostoyevski, used drugs and engaged in free love. Their decadent lifestyle appealed to the addictive side of Kerouac's personality (Charters notes that Kerouac once told Ginsberg that "benzedrine intensified his awareness and made him feel more clever") but he soon grew bored with what he called their "mental garbage of 'existentialism' and 'hipsterism' and 'bourgeois decadence.'" The son of a working-class family, Kerouac also found it difficult to relate to the spoiled antics (deliberately hurling plates of food to the floor in restaurants, tearing perfectly good clothing to shreds) of these sons of well-to-do parents.

Kerouac's mood darkened after his father's death from stomach cancer in the spring of 1946. He had failed to live up to Leo Kerouac's vision: football star, college graduate, navy hero. Instead, Jack had disgraced the family with his annulled marriage, drunkenness, drug addiction, and as yet unfulfilled hopes of becoming a writer. The only commitment to his father Kerouac could honor was to stay home and take care of *mémêre*, a promise he had made to Leo as the man died in his son's arms. In his melancholy, Kerouac began writing what would become his first published book, *The Town and the City* (1950). (Two earlier efforts at novels—one written with Burroughs—were unpublished.)

"I settled down to write in solitude, in pain, writing hymns and prayers," he relates in *Vanity*, hoping that in the process he would be "redeemed." As Charters notes, Kerouac's "talent as a writer was not his inventiveness with new characters and plots, but rather his power to dramatize the spirit of his own life into romantic fantasy." As such, the storyline of *The Town and the City*, as did most of his plots, closely paralelled the events of his life.

Towards the end of that year, Kerouac met the legendary Neal Cassady, who became his spritual brother and confidant. The free-spirited and volcanic Cassady became the model for Dean Moriarty, hero of *On the Road*, as well as Cody Pomeray who appears in *The Dharma Bums* (1958) among other books.

Kerouac had first heard tales of this "mad genius of jails and raw power" who was a "God among the girls" and a "reader of Schopenhauer in reform schools" from a friend at Columbia who had known Cassady in Colorado. The product of a broken home, Neal led a fairly lawless life growing up on the streets of Denver during the thirties and early forties. At fourteen, he developed a lifelong passion for driving automobiles and began joyriding in stolen cars. By the time he was twenty-one, he had stolen over 500 vehicles, been arrested almost a dozen times, and served several stretches in reform schools. It was during one of his incarcerations that he began reading philosophy. Following the somewhat crooked trail of his intellectual curiousity, he ended up in New York in the winter of 1946 (with his 16-year-old wife, Luanne, in tow) eager to rub elbows and exchange ideas with the Columbia hipster crowd he had heard about.

"[H]e was a young jailkid all hung-up on the wonderful possibilities of becoming a real intellectual," Kerouac wrote of Moriarty/Cassady in the opening chapter of *On the Road.* "[H]e liked to talk in the tone and using the words, but in a jumbled way, that he had heard from 'real intellectuals' . . ."

Cassady asked Kerouac to teach him to be a writer and often visited Jack when he was working. He would lie on the bed reading out loud or hover over Kerouac, whooping and bobbing in excitement:

> *He watched over my shoulder as I wrote strories, yelling "Yes! That's right! Wow! Man!" and "Phew!" and wiped his face with his handkerchief . . . And a kind of holy lightening I saw flashing from his excitement and his visions, which he described so torrentially that people in buses looked around to see the "overexcited nut."* (On the Road)

Yet while Cassady thought of himself as the pupil, Kerouac (speaking as narrator Sal Paradise in *On the Road*) admits that he "began to learn from him as much as he probably learned from me." Kerouac drew on Cassady's limitless energy and enthusiasm. It was Cassady who believed that writing should be read as "a continuous chain of undisciplined thought," which, as Charters observes, "became the basis of Kerouac's literary aesthetic of spontaneous prose." If Cassady was indeed an "overexcited nut," then he was all the more qualified to stimulate Kerouac's creativity, as narrator Sal Paradise relates in *On the Road*:

> *[T]he only people for me are the mad ones, the ones who are mad to live, mad to talk, mad to be saved, desirous of everything at the same time, the ones who never yawn or say a commonplace thing, but burn, burn, burn like fabulous yellow roman candles*

*exploding like spiders across the stars and in the middle you see
the blue centerlight pop and everybody goes "Awww!"*

Cassady returned to Denver in the spring of 1947 with
Luanne. Ginsberg, with whom Neal was romantically involved,
soon followed. Kerouac joined them all that summer, arriving
by bus after a failed attempt at hitchhiking cross-country. It
wasn't much of a reunion: Neal spent most of his time with
Ginsberg and a new girlfriend, Carolyn Robinson.

Keeping notes along the way, Kerouac continued on to San
Francisco and worked briefly as a security guard before heading down to Los Angeles. He picked cotton, lived with a
Chicano woman, then one day crammed his seaman's bag with
sandwiches and his notebooks and headed back east as far as
his money would take him, which turned out to be Pittsburgh.
By the time he reached New York, he was so broke he had to
panhandle the 25-cent bus fare to get home to Long Island.

After a relatively sedate year under his mother's roof, during
which time he worked on *The Town and the City* and began an
early draft of *On the Road*, he was off again, this time with
Cassady and Luanne in a brand-new silver Nash. They drove
to Louisiana to visit Burroughs, then pushed on to California.
This and subsequent trips with Cassady, together with notes
from the solo journey in California, provided much of the raw
material for *On the Road*.

Kerouac returned to New York in February of 1949 and a
month later received the happy news that Robert Giroux at
Harcourt Brace had accepted *The Town and the City*. The young
author was delighted about getting published but was horrified
when Giroux edited out two thirds of the 1,100-page manuscript. Still, Kerouc was confident that the book would make
him a fortune and he and Cassady plotted grand itineraries for
trips abroad during their third journey together—a riotous trek
from California to Chicago at breakneck speed, eventually
terminating at Kerouac's mother's new apartment in Queens.

Kerouac was crushed when *The Town and the City* received
mixed reviews upon publication in March of 1950. Sales

dropped off after only a few weeks and the disillusioned author set off once more with Cassady to visit Burroughs, who was now living in Mexico City. Cassady returned to the States after a week, but Kerouac, sick with amoebic dysentery, stayed on with Burroughs and his future wife Joan, who nursed the ailing author back to health.

Returning to New York in the fall, Kerouac stunned his friends and family by marrying twenty-year-old Joan Haverty, a woman he barely knew. She was the former girlfriend of one of Jack's old New York friends, Bill Cannastra, who had died in a subway accident.

Joan waitressed while Kerouac took a part-time job synopsizing novels for Twentieth Century Fox. In April of 1951, he began once more to work on the story of his travels with Cassady, which would later become *On the Road.* He was inspired by letters from Neal, one in particular known as the "Joan Anderson letter" in which Cassady describes some of his sexual exploits. Riotously bopping along for thousands upon thousands of words, "sometimes breathtaking in speed and brilliance" as Ginsberg put it, the Joan Anderson letter "was a godsend," according to biographer Dennis McNally, author of *Desolate Angel: Jack Kerouac, the Beat Generation, and America:* "[A] click of recognition in his inner ear . . . told [Kerouac] that *this* was the way to tell a story—just spontaneously tell it, allow it to flow out, assume its own shape, to use the infinite accretion of details as a form itself."

Loaded up on coffee and Benzedrine, Kerouac sat at his typewriter from early morning until late at night feverishly typing away. Hating to stop even long enough to change typing paper, he pasted together long sheets of Chinese art paper and fed the roll through the carriage of his typewriter. His one distraction was the breakup of his marriage to Joan. Fed up with her husband's self-indulgence and lack of gainful employment, she threw Kerouac out and he moved in with friend Lucien Carr. Continuing his typing on a roll of teletype paper which Carr brought home from his job at UPI, Kerouac completed *On the Road* in just under three weeks. The

175,000-word manuscript, recalled fellow Beat writer John Clellon Holmes (as quoted by Charters) was "a scroll three inches thick made up of one single-spaced, unbroken paragraph 120 feet long . . . [I] knew immediately it was the best thing he had done."

Unfortunately, the editors at Harcourt Brace did not agree and rejected the manuscript. It took six more years for *On the Road* to appear in print. Emotionally as well as physically drained, Kerouac suffered a flare-up of thrombophlebitis in his legs and was confined to a hospital bed for several weeks. Meanwhile, Joan had news for him: she was pregnant. Kerouac vehemently denied that he was the father and for years refused to pay child support. The child, Jan Kerouac, eventually became a novelist herself.

During his confinement in the hospital, Kerouac immersed himself in the works of turn-of-the-century French novelist Marcel Proust. Inspired by Proust's voluminous autobiographical masterpiece *Remembrance of Things Past,* Kerouac heard the "ghosts of the Pawtucketville night" beckoning and envisioned his own multi-volume autobiography. He also began to seek a new direction for his writing—a "deep form," as he put it, which would meld the rollicking "horizontal" narrative movement of *On the Road* with the "vertical" depth of his more reflective writing.

Kerouac discovered his form in the improvisational, free-floating saxophone solos of such jazz legends as Charlie Parker and Lee Konitz. He wished to produce the literary equivalent of this music, a "flow of words and the releasing bop-sound at the end of a prose rhythm paragraph." He found the means through a spontaneous form of composition which he called "sketching." Kerouac took his cue from an artist friend, Ed White, who suggested that he "sketch in the streets like a painter but with words." Notebook and pencil ever in hand and a copy of Proust in his pocket, the excited author began wandering about New York, sketching everything he saw.

"You just have to purify your mind and let it pour words," he told Ginsberg. "[W]rite with 100 percent personal honesty . . . and slap it all down shameless, willynilly, rapidly."

Kerouac regrettably understood that his new style lacked commercial appeal but was nevertheless convinced that it was the only way to write. He "had found his voice at last," according to Charters: "For Jack the appeal of sketching was his excitement letting himself go on paper, just as a jazz musician blew riff after riff of a solo following whatever direction his own mind and immediate emotions led him."

Kerouac's next writing project, *Visions of Cody* (1959), provides some of the finest examples of his literary "sketches." Originally titled *Visions of Neal, Visions of Cody* is ostensibly the story of Cassady's youth, but is "really Kerouac's dream image of himself," according to Charters. Writing *Visions* prepared Kerouac for the Proustian task of composing his own series of autobiographical novels, beginning with *Doctor Sax* (1959), the story of his adolesence in Lowell:

> *The other night I had a dream that I was sitting on the sidewalk on Moody Street, Pawtucketville, Lowell, Mass., with a pencil and paper in my hand saying to myself "Describe the wrinkly tar of this sidewalk, also the iron pickets of Textile Institute, or the doorway where Lousy and you and G. J.'s always sittin and dont stop to think of words when you do stop, just stop to think of the picture better—and let your mind off yourself in this work."*

Doctor Sax is one of the many shadowy figures haunting this dark, experimental novel of sexual tension, confusion, and coming of age in a French-Canadian New England factory town. Jack Duluoz is the narrator/Kerouac character and Kerouac subsequently referred to the entire series as "The Legend of Duluoz"—"a prolonged search for a lost identity," as Charters notes. The Duluoz novels include *The Subterraneans* (1958), *Maggie Cassidy, Tristessa* (1960), *Big Sur* (1962), *Visions of Gerard,* and *Desolation Angels* (1965).

Kerouac wrote these and several other works (some unpublished) between 1951 and 1957 in a remarkably sustained burst

Kerouac's boyhood home in Lowell, Massachusetts (multi-family house on corner, above Pepsi sign), where "the wrinkly tar of [the] sidewalk" and "the iron pickets" of the textile mills would later inspire many of the autobiographical novels of his "Duluoz" series, such as Doctor Sax *and* Visions of Gerard.
(Tom Verde)

of creativity. He reputedly composed *The Subterraneans,* for instance, in just 72 hours. He also did much of this writing "on the road" as it were, as he crisscrossed the country hopping freight trains, hitchhiking, working as a railroad brakeman, a deck hand, even a fire lookout on Desolation Mountain in Washington state's Mount Baker National Forest.

He spent January through May of 1952 living in San Franciso with Cassady, who by then had married Carolyn Robinson. The friendship between Kerouac and Cassady began to deteriorate after several months and Kerouac left for Mexico, where he visited Burroughs and worked on *Doctor Sax*. He returned to his mother's for Christmas and spent six weeks writing *Maggie Cassidy* (originally *Springtime Mary*), the story of one of his teenage love affairs in Lowell. Kerouac hoped that the book's relatively straightfoward narrative would appeal to publishers, but, like *On the Road* and *Visions of Cody*, it was initially rejected.

One fortunate break at this time was a lunchtime meeting with the influential critic and poet Malcolm Cowley, an editorial adviser to Viking Press. Cowley thought *Doctor Sax* and *Visions of Cody* were too experimental for mainstream publishers but was impressed with *On the Road*. Still, Cowley said he couldn't promise anything and Kerouac left the table without much of a commitment from Viking, but sufficiently drunk on the free martinis.

Kerouac and the Cassadys were briefly reunited in San Jose, California, but the relationship between Jack and Neal was effectively over. Kerouac was also on bad terms with Burroughs and Ginsberg after the poet criticized *Doctor Sax*. On top of it all, most of his works remained unpublished and his ex-wife Joan was suing him for child support. The strain began to take its toll. He sunk into a deep depression and retreated once more to the familar haven of his mother's apartment in Queens where he holed up in his room, drinking, smoking marijuana, and feeling suicidal.

His spirit was somewhat lifted early in 1954, resulting from a trip to the local public library. While reading Thoreau, he came upon a reference to Hinduism which led him to study the life of Buddha. He embarked on a path of Zen monasticism, poring over Buddhist texts, planting a garden, meditating, and practicing celibacy. His asceticism was short-lived, however. Tempted by the lure of the bottle, he soon reverted to his old vices.

That spring, thanks to Cowley's influence, *New World Writing* magazine bought an excerpt from *On the Road*; the $120 check was the first money Kerouac had received for his writing in four years. Cowley also boosted Jack's reputation in the pages of the *Saturday Review* by crediting him with coining the term "the Beat Generation" and calling the yet-unpublished *On the Road* "the best record of their lives."

It was a record that was beginning to enjoy increased recognition. In 1952, Scribner's had published *Go*, a novel based on the experiences of Kerouac, Cassady, and the rest of the Beats written by Kerouac's friend John Clellon Holmes. That same year Holmes also wrote a Sunday *New York Times* magazine article entitled "This Is the Beat Generation" and the term officially entered the lexicon of mainstream America.[*] But it was Ginsberg, in October of 1955, who eloquently captured the voice of the Beat movement when he performed a reading of his new poem, "Howl," in a San Francisco nightclub—a reading which Kerouac attended.

During this period, Kerouac was beginning to gain some attention himself, due to the publication of his *On the Road* excerpt, which appeared under the title "Jazz of the Beat Generation," in *New World Writing*. Another excerpt ("The Mexican Girl") from an earlier version of *Road* appeared in *The Paris Review* at about the same time and the editors at Viking, as Cowley had predicted, actively renewed interest in *On the Road*. In December of 1956, Kerouac's career took a fateful turn when Viking finally offered him a contract and a $1,000 advance for the book. Less than a year later, *On the Road* was published.

Despite a number of criticisms—"infantile," "wild and incomprehensible," "lack[ing] seriousness," and the like—from some reviewers, the revered gray lady of journalism, *The New York Times*, bestowed its influential blessing on the book by christening it a "major novel." *Times* reviewer Gilbert Millstein compared *On the Road* to Hemingway's *The Sun Also Rises* as

---

[*] "Beat" was a popular slang term among jazz musicians and drug dealers in the post–World War II years. Originally meaning poor or exhausted ("Man, I'm beat"), the word was adopted by the Columbia crowd—Burroughs, Ginsberg, Carr, Kerouac, et al.—and came to mean someone or something existing on the edge of society, a noncomformist or a rebel in search of a "New Vision" of art and truth. In the wake of the 1958 launching of the Russian Sputnik satellite, a columnist for the *San Francisco Chronicle* playfully coined the term "beatniks" and disciples of the Beat Generation had a name.

a generational statement: "The most beautifully executed, the clearest and most important utterance yet made by the generation Kerouac himself named 'beat' . . ."

Yet critical regard, one way or the other, meant little to *On the Road*'s most enthusiatic and enduring audience, i.e. the youth of America. The book spoke directly to them, unimpeded by the conventional academic analyses or endorsements which often accompany "the classics." "The young people who responded to the book, who read it not as 'literature' but as an adventure, recognized that Kerouac was on their side, the side of youth and freedom . . . the chance to be yourself," wrote Charters. While this yearning for self-expression and individualism became a rallying cry of the radical sixties counterculture, the character of Moriarty/Cassady as an idealogical American hero has a much longer pedigree. "Kerouac's vision of Neal Cassady . . . centered in one of the most vital fantasies of America, the dream of the cowboy, free and footloose," observed Charters. As such, Moriarty/Cassady is the classic American folk hero, "a drifter" imbued with "the spirit of the wide, western plains" who seeks to escape "the crowding and commercialization of modern life."

On the Road went into its second printing just two weeks after its release and stayed on the best-seller list for over a month. Lucrative offers for articles about the Beat Generation were pouring in from *Esquire, Playboy,* and others. Actress Lillian Hellman commissioned Kerouac to write a play; there was talk of a huge deal from Warner Brothers and of casting Marlon Brando in a film version of *On the Road.* Hollywood, meanwhile, paid $15,000—more money than Jack had ever made on a single sale—for the rights to *The Subterraneans.* New York intellectuals, eager to be hip, threw pretentious literary parties for him; there were television interviews with hard-nosed journalists like Mike Wallace who appeared to have trouble understanding what the so-called spokesman for the Beat Generation was talking about; and burgeoning numbers of fans.

Kerouac was ill-prepared for this sudden onslaught of fame, even though he had been struggling for years to attain it. He characteristically sought refuge behind a bottle ("my liquid suit of armor" as he called it) and the media-proof doors of his mother's house. But his public refused to leave him alone. "Without asking him," observed biographer Tom Clark, "the national media had appointed him the spokesman for an entire generation, and his slightest thoughts made the wires hum from coast to coast."

Viking was pressuring him for a follow-up to *On the Road* and he responded by cranking out *The Dharma Bums* in just ten sittings. The book picks up where *Road* left off, with a Bohemian group of friends heading into the mountains out west in search of truth and the Zen path to enlightenment. Written, like *Road*, on a continuous roll of paper, *Dharma Bums* has the same narrative pitch and roll to it. Right from the start, the reader can almost feel the tug of the train and hear the miles clacking away beneath the weight of the freight car:

> *Hopping a freight out of Los Angeles at high noon one day in late September 1955 I got on a gondola and lay down with my duffel bag under my head and my knees crossed and contemplated the clouds as we rolled north to Santa Barbara.*

Even though Kerouac announces in the opening chapter that he was once an "oldtime bhikku in modern clothes wandering the world . . . in order to turn the wheel of True Meaning, or Dharma, and gain merit for [him]self as a future Buddha (Awakener)," he confesses that he has since become "a little tired and cynical." He was in fact not overly enthused with *Dharma Bums*, and considered it a "potboiler"—something he wrote to simply pay for the rent, his liquor habit, and food for the cat. He still considered his experimental fiction, such as *Doctor Sax* or *Visions of Cody*, to be his best work and was frustrated that others did not agree.

The critics, though, were becoming increasingly hostile, labeling Kerouac's books "incoherent" and unreadable. John Updike took a stinging swipe at *Road* in the pages of *The New*

Yorker with a parody entitled "On the Sidewalk"; Columbia academic Robert Brustein pilloried Kerouac's new American hero as "inarticulate" while author Truman Capote delivered one of the most memorable Kerouac-bashing barbs when he sneered: "Writing! That's not writing, it's just . . . typing!"

Kerouac was as ill equipped to handle such disdain as he had been to cope with success. By the summer of 1960, the pressure drove him into a self-imposed solitary confinement near Big Sur, California, in a cabin that belonged to friend and Beat poet Lawrence Ferlinghetti. Here, alone in the wilderness, Kerouac reached and fell off the edge of a nervous breakdown which he chronicled two years later in *Big Sur*, another in the Duluoz series of novels.

Kerouac spent the next several years traveling, taking care of his mother, who suffered a stroke in 1966, and literally drinking himself to death. The same year his mother had her stroke, he married Stella Sampas, the sister of an old family friend, and moved back to Lowell. She and her family tried to protect Jack from the outside world and himself, but he was too strongly bent on self-destruction to be helped.

Two years later, in February of 1968, Kerouac received the devastating news that Cassady was dead. Kerouac's "hero of the pure snowy wild West" had mixed too many drugs with too much alcohol at a wedding in Mexico and was found lying on a railroad track, dead of congestive heart failure. Jack was so overwhelmed that for months he refused to believe that his old friend was actually gone and not just hiding out somewhere. In the fall of that year, Kerouac appeared on the television show "Firing Line" hosted by William F. Buckley. On the program, for which he had prepared himself by drinking whiskey and smoking marijuana all day, Kerouac belligerently denounced Ginsberg and the Beats with slurred and angry words. He never saw nor spoke to any of his old friends again.

He fled with his family to St. Petersburg, Florida, where they were so destitute that Stella had to take a menial $2-an-hour job to support them all. The end came in the fall of 1969. On the morning of October 20, Kerouac was sitting in front of the television drinking his usual breakfast of whiskey and beer when he felt a sudden pain in his abdoman and began vomiting blood. Stella rushed him to the hospital, where surgeons struggled for eighteen hours to keep him alive. He died at 5:30 A.M., on October 21, 1969, from a massive internal hemorrhage brought on by cirrhosis of the liver. He was forty-seven years old.

On the Road and *The Dharma Bums* remain Kerouac's best-known works, while as a literary figure he is most often credited with helping to ignite the cultural revolution of the 1960s. Many of the most famous rebels who strode through the limelight of that era—Marlon Brando, James Dean, Elvis Presley, Lenny Bruce, Bob Dylan, Abbie Hoffman, Jerry Rubin, Timothy Leary—sprang, to one degree or another, from the seeds sown by Kerouac and the Beats during the comparatively complacent Eisenhower years.

Yet Kerouac would be the first to deny that he was an iconoclast, an idol smasher who hammered away at the temples of the establishment simply for the sake of self-satisfied change. Ever a son of the Roman Catholic church, to him the word "beat" did not mean "cool" so much as it meant "beatific" (blessed) or "in a state of beatitude . . . trying to love all life." In the wake of his skyrocketing fame, he consistently rejected the notion that his influence had anything to do whatsoever with the antiwar movement, LSD, Woodstock, the Merry Pranksters, the 1968 Democratic National Convention, or even the Beats themselves.

Rather than siring "a deluge of alienated radicals, war protestors, dropouts, [and] hippies," as he put it in one of his last non-posthumously published pieces—the essay "After Me, the Deluge," written for *The Chicago Tribune*—he wished to be remembered only as an artist and "the intellectual forbear of modern spontaneous prose." While spontaneous prose did not, as he predicted, come to dominate the literary landscape of the future, Kerouac's artistic legacy can be traced through such modern authors as Ken Kesey, Tom Wolfe, Tom Robbins, and, for that matter, all practicioners of a highly personalized, freestyle reporting method which became known as "The New Journalism."

Chronology

March 12, 1922	born Jean Louis Lebris de Kerouac in Lowell, Massachusetts
1939	graduates Lowell High School, a football star
1939–40	attends Horace Mann School in New York City; makes up courses he failed at Lowell to qualify for football scholarship to Columbia University
1940–41	attends Columbia College but drops out in sophomore year
1942–43	joins navy, merchant marine
1944	marries art student Edie Parker but marriage only lasts a few months; through Parker, meets Allen Ginsberg, William Burroughs, and Lucien Carr
1946	starts writing *The Town and the City*; meets Neal Cassady
1947–50	first cross-country trips with Cassady; makes notes for *On the Road*
1950	first novel, *The Town and the City,* published; marries Joan Haverty, but marriage ends after six months
1951	fueled by coffee and Benzedrine, writes *On the Road* in three-week marathon on single roll of paper; Harcourt Brace rejects manuscript; is confined to hospital bed with thrombophlebitis

1952	daughter Michelle Jan Kerouac born; denies paternity; begins experimenting with "spontaneous prose"
1953–54	back and forth between New York and San Francisco; writes *Maggie Cassidy* and *The Subterraneans*
1955	taken to court by Haverty for not paying child support; historic reading of Ginsberg's "Howl" at Six Gallery in San Francisco
1957	*On the Road*
1958	*The Dharma Bums*; *The Subterraneans*
1959	*Maggie Cassidy; Doctor Sax*
1966	marries Stella Sampas
1968	Neal Cassady dies; *Vanity of Duluoz*
October 21, 1969	dies in St. Petersburg, Florida from a massive internal hemorrhage brought on by cirrhosis of the liver
1972	*Visions of Cody*

Further Reading

Kerouac's Works

On the Road (New York: Penguin Books, 1991). Kerouac's most famous novel and the book that established him as a major American literary figure. This particular edition includes a detailed and insightful introduction by leading Beat scholar Ann Charters.

Visions of Cody (New York: McGraw-Hill Book Company, 1972). Experimental biography of Neal Cassady, includes best examples of Kerouac's spontaneous prose style, or "sketching"; introduction by Allen Ginsberg.

Vanity of Duluoz (New York: Coward-McCann, 1968). A young Franco-American's early days in a New England facory town; one in a series of autobiographical "Duluoz" novels

The Dharma Bums (New York: Viking, 1958). Kerouac's followup to *On the Road*.

The Portable Jack Kerouac, edited by Ann Charters (New York: Viking, 1995). Selections from Kerouac's majors works, essays, poetry, and letters, covering everything from the Beat Generation to Buddhism; includes chronology and commentary on the texts throughout by Charters. An excellent resource.

Books About Kerouac

Carolyn Cassady, *Off the Road: My Years with Cassady, Kerouac, and Ginsberg* (New York: William Morrow and Company, Inc. 1990). Deeply personal, detailed, and authoritative account by Cassady's widow. Provides unique insights into the lives of various members of the Beat Generation.

Ann Charters, *Kerouac: A Biography* (New York: St. Martin's Press, 1973). The definitive adult biography of Kerouac written by one of the leading Beat scholars in America, who also happened to know and work with Kerouac, Ginsberg, and many of the other Beats. Includes a bibliographical chronology of Kerouac's books as well as a key to the true identity of various characters in the novels.

Ann Charters, editor, *The Portable Beat Reader* (New York: Viking Press, 1992). Thorough overview of the Beats, with extensive commentary throughout by Charters. An excellent resource.

Tom Clark, *Jack Kerouac* (San Diego, New York, London: Harcourt Brace Jovanovich, 1984). Lively, alternative biography, generously illustrated. Includes a bibliography of primary and secondary sources.

Warren French, *Jack Kerouac: Novelist of the Beat Generation* (Boston: Twayne Publishers, 1986). Good, concise biographical criticism.

Dennis McNally, *Desolate Angel: Jack Kerouac, the Beat Generation* (New York: Random House, 1979). Colorfully written and personal account of Kerouac's life as well as the era.

Kurt Vonnegut
(1922–)

Unwillingly pigeonholed as a science-fiction writer, Kurt Vonnegut spent years confined to the paperback trade as an underground author before being recognized as one of the most daring, innovative, and popular authors of our time. He claims that he was misunderstood simply because he happened to "notice technology" in his books.
(National Archives)

*F*ive days after his fifty-sixth birthday, writer Kurt Vonnegut received a letter from an Indiana high-school student. Having read nearly everything Vonnegut ever wrote, the devoted young fan concluded that the collective works of his literary hero boiled down to this simple maxim: "Love may fail, but courtesy will prevail."

Vonnegut wholeheartedly agreed, as he relates in the prologue to his ninth novel, *Jailbird* (1979). "I am now in the abashed condition . . . of realizing that I needn't have bothered to write several books," he observed. "A seven-word telegram would have done the job. Seriously."

Such is the jocular, self-effacing attitude of one of the most daring, innovative, and popular authors of our time. Yet he is also perhaps one of American literature's most misunderstood. Pigeonholed, and largely dismissed, for years as a science-fiction and/or underground writer, Vonnegut has broken free of those molds in recent decades and gained the critical attention he deserves. An avowed anti-intellectual, this descendent of German immigrants has remained true to his solid, midwestern, middle-class background and to his essential outlook on modern life, whether in this world or on some futuristic and distant planet: that human beings ought not to be valued by what or how much they produce, but for the simple fact that they *are* human beings and as such deserve to be treated with dignity.

Vonnegut has made his plea for respect for the human race, as well as its preservation, over the course of four increasingly mechanized, highly technological decades of modern American life. It might seem ironic that an author who has written about extraterrestrial visitations and time travel should in the same breath speak out against the space program or caution us, as he did in *God Bless You, Mr. Rosewater* (1965), about "the sophistication of machines." Yet it is not technology itself which Vonnegut finds threatening—only its misuse.

"I thought scientists were going to find out exactly how everything worked, and then make it work better," he told the 1970 graduating class of Bennington College. "Scientific truth was going to make us so happy and comfortable. What actually happened when I was twenty-one was that we dropped scientific truth on Hiroshima. We killed everybody there. And I had just come home from being a prisoner of war in Dresden, which I'd seen burned to the ground . . . I have been a consistent pessimist ever since . . ."

Vonnegut recognized in technology its potential to threaten civilization in much subtler ways, gradually fraying the fabric of our culture. "This is a lonesome society . . . fragmented by the factory system," he once told an interviewer. "People have to move from here to there as jobs move, as prosperity leaves one area and appears somewhere else. People don't live in communities permanently anymore. But they should: Communities are very comforting to human beings."

Vonnegut once knew the comfort of such a community and home life, and knew also the feeling of having them wrenched away. The third child of Kurt and Edith (Lieber) Vonnegut was born on November 11, 1922, in Indianapolis, Indiana and was named Kurt Jr., after his father. The Vonneguts and the Liebers had been in Indianapolis for almost a century, having come to America during the great wave of German immigration during the mid-nineteeth century. The Liebers made a fortune in brewing while Vonnegut's grandfather, Bernard, became a prominent architect, as did his son, Kurt Sr. Both the Vonneguts and the Liebers were cultured families, with a high regard for the fine arts, especially German poetry and music, and a deep respect for their German heritage.

Vonnegut's older siblings—brother Bernard and sister Alice—grew up in a world of governesses and private schools. By the time of Kurt Jr.'s birth in the early twenties, however, life had changed for the Vonneguts as well as every other German-American family in the United States. Anti-German prejudice swept the country in the wake of World War I and the "delight" which the Vonneguts derived from their cultural background was "permanently crippled," as Vonnegut relates in *Slapstick* (1976): "Children in our family were no longer taught German. Neither were they encouraged to admire German music or literature or art or science. My brother and sister and I were raised as though Germany were as foreign to us as Paraguay . . . And our family became a lot less interesting, especially to itself."

During the 1920s, the eighteenth amendment to the Constitution outlawing the sale or manufacture of liquor

(Prohibition) cut short the Lieber brewing income. The Great Depression that followed in 1929 severely hindered the building industry, effectively putting Vonnegut's architect father out of business. In 1937, the Vonneguts were forced to moved from their large brick house on Illinois Street to a more modest residence in the suburbs. Unable to find work over the next ten years, Kurt Sr. became increasingly withdrawn while Edith Vonnegut, accustomed to a luxurious lifestyle, suffered the humiliation of having to sell family heirlooms to help make ends meet. She took some writing courses and attempted to sell stories to magazines in order to bring in some money. None of her stories were ever published, but her efforts and determination made a strong impact on her youngest son.

Resentful over her husband's lack of employment, Edith Vonnegut grew bitter as the years wore on. She started drinking heavily, and eventually committed suicide in 1944 by overdosing on sleeping pills. It took years for Vonnegut and his family to speak openly about the fact that Edith had taken her own life. As her son notes with bittersweet candor in the prologue to *Jailbird*, "[m]y mother . . . had declined to go on living, since she could no longer be what she had been at the time of her marriage—one of the richest women in town."

Another important influence during these troubled times was humor, which could be had for a quarter down at the local movie house or tuned in each evening via radio.

"When people ask me who my cultural heroes are," Vonnegut once wrote, "I express pious gratitude for Mark Twain and James Joyce and so on. But the truth is that I am a barbarian, whose deepest cultural debts are to Laurel and Hardy, Stoopnagel and Bud, Buster Keaton, Fred Allen, Jack Benny, Charlie Chaplin, Easy Aces, Henry Morgan, and so on. They made me hilarious during the Great Depression, and all the lesser depressions after that."

Vonnegut's incisive and somewhat offbeat sense of humor, cultivated in part by his exposure to these comedic stars of yesteryear, is evident in such seminal works as *God Bless You, Mr. Rosewater, Cat's Cradle* (1963), *Mother Night* (1962) and

Breakfast of Champions (1973); his sense of humor continues to percolate through the more recent novels, essays, and other writings.

After graduating from Shortridge High School, where he was a correspondent for the school newspaper, Vonnegut entered the 1940 freshman class of Cornell University as a chemistry major. He spent most of his time lounging about the offices of *The Cornell Daily Sun,* instead of studying chemistry, however. He became the *Sun's* managing editor and ended up writing a regular column, in which he began to develop his writer's voice.

Vonnegut also devoted time to delving into the works of Mark Twain, as well as H. G. Wells, Robert Louis Stevenson, and George Bernard Shaw in addition to pulling some rather creative college pranks. One of his favorites was to attend the final exam of a large course in which he was not enrolled, stand up, tear the exam to pieces and hurl them into the astonished professor's face before slamming the door behind him. On another occasion he appeared at an ROTC inspection (ROTC was a required credit at the time, and about the only course Vonnegut wasn't flunking) "wearing every sort of medal, for swimming, for scouting, for Sunday-school attendance" that he could lay his hands on, as he recalled in his 1991 memoir, *Fates Worse Than Death.*

The jokes ended in March of 1943 when Vonnegut enlisted in the army and was sent to the Carnegie Institute of Technology and the University of Tennessee to study mechanical engineering. The news of his enlistment came as a blow to his mother, who was afraid she would lose her son to a war which she opposed. Vonnegut returned home on leave in May of 1944 to see her on Mother's Day, but she died the night before he arrived. In November he joined the 106th Infantry Division in England and fought in the Battle of the Bulge, where he was captured by the Germans on December 22.

He and his fellow POWs were taken to Dresden, a city rich in architectural treasures and which was supposedly "open," i.e. safe from Allied attack because of its lack of troops and war production facilities. But on the night of February 13, 1945,

British and American planes firebombed Dresden in a cataclys-
mic attack which reduced the city to a smoldering pile of
rubble. The attack was an act of terror, intended to crush the
Germans' fighting spirit; 135,000 civilians were killed by the
bombing (some estimates run as high as 200,000)—the biggest
massacre in European history and twice the number of casu-
alties at Hiroshima. Vonnegut and his fellow POWs survived
the attack by taking shelter in an underground meat locker.

"When we came up again, the city was gone and everybody
was dead—a terrible thing for the son of an architect to see..."
he recalled in a talk given at the University of Iowa. Even more
terrible was the task of hauling the charred remains of the dead
from the ruins, as Vonnegut related in the introduction to
Mother Night: "[W]e were put to work as corpse miners, breaking into shelters, bringing bodies out. And I got to see many
German types of all ages as death had found them, usually with
valuables in their laps. Sometimes relatives would come and
watch us dig."

The insane horror and absurdity of Dresden were etched
deeply onto Vonnegut's psyche. These "German types" which
he dragged from the rubble could very well have been his
relatives. Furthermore, he saw what his own side was capable
of and had to wonder, as scholar Peter Reed observed, if this
was the act of the "good guys." Brought up to believe that
science and technology would benefit civilization, Vonnegut
instead watched them "destroy, in fourteen hours, a thousand-
year-old city, a symbol of man's cooperation, a monument to
his nobility," as scholar John Somer notes in *The Vonnegut
Statement.*

Vonnegut would spend the next 23 years of his life trying to
come to terms with Dresden, gradually approaching the subject in his early books until finally confronting it head on in the
milestone work that marked a turning point in his career,
Slaughterhouse Five (1969).

---

*A collection of critical essays by various authors on Vonnegut's life and works
(see bibliography).

Upon his return from the war, Vonnegut married his childhood sweetheart, Jane Marie Cox, in September of 1945. He enrolled as a graduate student in anthropology at the University of Chicago and also worked as a cub reporter for the Chicago City News Bureau, covering the police beat. As with the *Cornell Sun,* the regular routine of writing finished prose every day helped develop his style as a fiction writer.

Vonnegut left Chicago three years later without a degree after the anthropology department unanimously rejected his thesis, *Fluctuations Between Good and Evil in Simple Tales,* as unscientific. He joined his scientist brother, Bernard, in the research lab at General Electric Corporation in Schenectady, New York—not as a researcher, but as a public relations official. The job offered security and enabled him to draw on his journalistic experience while catering to his scientific interests.

An artist by nature, however, Vonnegut soon found the business of public relations "disagreeable." He disliked having to sometimes disguise the truth in the line of duty. And while fascinated by the technological advances being made at GE he was uncomfortable with their implications. He was all for the advancement of science—he just objected to it advancing too rapidly over the lives of people.

And so Vonnegut began writing stories and then a novel about what he saw happening to the world, through the lens of the research lab at GE. He sold his first story, "Report on the Barnhouse Effect," to *Collier's* in 1949 (the story appeared in February of 1950). Other sales followed to many of the popular magazines such as *Esquire, Ladies' Home Journal, The Saturday Evening Post,* and *Cosmopolitan.* These publications paid upwards of $2,700 per story and it began to occur to Vonnegut that, as a regular contributor, he just might be able to make a living as a writer.

With a half dozen or so story sales to his credit and a book contract from Scribner's in hand, the aspiring author felt confident enough in 1951 to quit his job at GE and move to Cape Cod, Massachusetts, where he devoted most of his time

The General Electric research plant in Schenectady, New York, where Vonnegut worked as a public-relations official before quitting to become a writer. The then ultra-modern facility inspired the setting for his first novel, Player Piano.
(Courtesy General Electric Co.)

to writing. He supplemented his income by producing occasional ad copy and also ran the first Saab dealership in the area. It was a modest living but enough to support his family, which included three children, Mark, Nanette, and Edith.

His first novel, *Player Piano* (1952), came out of his experiences at GE. Paul Proteus is the protagonist of this futuristic book, set in the post–World War III city of Ilium, NY, in which most people have been put out of work by machines and human destiny is determined by computerized "National General Classification Tests" and "Achievement and Aptitude Profiles."

What reviews there were of *Player Piano* were mixed. Many mainstream critics simply ignored the book altogether, labeling it science fiction, a genre which they considered unworthy of serious critical consideration. The novel was reissued as a

Doubleday Science Fiction Book Club selection in 1953 and as a Bantam paperback the following year, under the new title *Utopia 14*. The new editions increased sales but further pegged Vonnegut as a science-fiction writer, a categorization he resisted.

"I learned from the reviewers that I was a science-fiction writer," he declared in an essay for *The New York Times Book Review*. "I didn't know that. I supposed I was writing a novel about life, about things I could not avoid seeing and hearing in Schenectady, a very real town, awkwardly set in the gruesome now. I have been a soreheaded occupant of a file drawer labeled 'science fiction' ever since, and I would like out, particularly since so many serious critics regularly mistake the drawer for a urinal."

The best way for a writer to get filed in that drawer, Vonnegut went on to complain, "is to notice technology. The feeling persists that no one can simultaneously be a respectable writer and understand how a refrigerator works . . ."

Vonnegut continued to write for the popular magazines, or *slicks*, as they were also called, throughout the fifties. It would be another seven years before he published his next book and he later characterized his short fiction as material he produced merely to finance the writing of his novels. Yet, as scholar Peter J. Reed observed, Vonnegut's short fiction does not "deserve such easy dismissal." The stories, Reed claims, were the product of Vonnegut's apprenticeship in fiction, and "are frequently tinged with sentimentality and nostalgia, traits that reappear in the novels . . ."

Appearing in the slicks also put Vonnegut in touch with various helpful people in the publishing world, such as *Collier's* editor Knox Burger who, in turn, introduced him to literary agent Kenneth Littauer. It was Littauer, Vonnegut once claimed, who taught him narrative structure and how to write a story, with a beginning, middle, and end.

Despite Littauer's influence, however, Vonnegut remained trapped in the science-fiction file drawer. It didn't help his image any when he was forced to sell some of the stories that the slicks had rejected to such sci-fi pulps as *The Magazine of Fantasy and Science Fiction, Galaxy,* and *Worlds of If.* Worse yet, his sci-fi label barred him from the desks of mainstream, hardcover book publishers, who had no interest in science fiction. Thus, his next few books, *The Sirens of Titan* (1959), the short fiction collection *Canary in a Cat House* (1961), and *Mother Night* were all published as paperback originals, meaning that they went unreviewed and were relegated to the obscurity of supermarket and drugstore book racks.

Of these early works, *The Sirens of Titan* is generally considered the best and the story of the book's creation has become part of the Vonnegut folklore. Encountering the author at a cocktail party, Knox Burger asked Vonnegut if he had any ideas for a new novel. "I had no ideas at all for a book," Vonnegut recalled later, but said that he just "started talking" and gave birth to the plot of *Sirens* there on the spot.

The Sirens of Titan is the closest Vonnegut has ever come to producing a pure science-fiction novel. Readers might ask why an author who was adamantly opposed to being called a science fiction writer would produce a book steeped in so many classic sci-fi/fantasy techniques, i.e., time/space travel, malicious Martians, robots, globe-conquering schemes, extraterrestrials, even giant moon birds (the huge bluebirds of Titan). *Sirens* is so rich in all of these elements that it is almost a "space opera," a formulaic subspecies of the sci-fi genre which is closer to a comic book than a novel in its depth and complexity.

Yet, one must consider the source. Vonnegut is a consummate jokester and *Sirens* is one of his best jokes. On one level, it is a parody of the campiest space operas, and as a work of humor succeeds as such. But Vonnegut is also an artist, and thus *Sirens of Titan* is something more than just a spoof.

By suggesting that the entire history of the world has been to no purpose other than to let some alien robot stranded on a desert moon know that a spare part for his spaceship is on its way, Vonnegut is ridiculing "mankind's obsession with finding an answer to the mystery of existence" outside of itself via a

Deity, according to scholar Donald L. Lawler. Since questions about the meaning of life are "unanswerable by their nature," Lawler goes on to observe in his essay on *Sirens*.[*] Vonnegut is telling us that an absurd solution like the plot of *Sirens* is just as plausible as the "big eye in the sky" or any other religious/philosophical explanation. This is not to say that Vonnegut considers human life absurd, Lawler notes, "only man's attempt to find an objective meaning to life."

The grafting of the science-fiction motif onto the ageless question of the meaning and nature of human destiny elevates Vonnegut and *Sirens* to the realm of serious literature for a number of reasons. In the first place, by using the space opera as an "enabling form," as Lawler puts it, Vonnegut joins the company of such noted predecessors as Mark Twain and Jonathan Swift, who used science fiction and fantasy to their own satirical and comedic ends in such works as *A Connecticut Yankee in King Arthur's Court* and *Gulliver's Travels*.

Secondly, producing a "new answer to the old question," as Karen and Charles Wood observe in *The Vonnegut Statement*, "is a necessary function of modern literature." Vonnegut's news is that "man at this point on his way toward his ultimate destiny doesn't know what that destiny is." Nor does he need to. Vonnegut "sees no need for absolute answers," the Woods claim, "Irresolution needs no resolution, but should rather be appreciated as the ultimate reality." Such insight into "man's bewilderment," they go on to say, "adds a dimension to Vonnegut's work which is missing in most of our previous literature."

But no such words of lofty praise were being written about Vonnegut in 1959, the year *Sirens* was published. Its paperbound spine and lurid, space-opera cover illustration were guaranteed to keep the book unnoticed by the critics and even out of most libraries. There was at least one silver lining: Samuel Stewart, who had been with the Western Printing Company, producers of *Sirens*, moved to the hardcover pub-

---

[*]Lawler's examination of *The Sirens of Titan* is included in *Vonnegut in America*, a collection of critical essays on Vonnegut's life and works (see bibliography).

lisher, Holt, Rinehart & Winston, where he was able to help Vonnegut secure a two-book contract.

This good news came at a welcome time. By the end of the decade, the popular magazines such as *Collier's* and *Saturday Evening Post*, which had been Vonnegut's bread and butter throughout the fifties, were folding, leaving him without a regular income. There were also tragic, personal losses. The death of Vonnegut's father in 1957 plunged the author into a year-long depression and writer's block; the following year, both his brother-in-law and his sister died within two days of each other, he in a train accident and she of cancer. Vonnegut adopted the eldest three of their four children (the youngest, an infant, went to a first cousin) and his financial pressures mounted.

With the publication of *Cat's Cradle* in 1963, Vonnegut's career gradually began to turn around. Strikingly original, the book takes on every known convention, from religion to science to politics and philosophy. Vonnegut stretched his creative limbs in this satirical and apocalyptic novel about the search for a mysterious substance that could end the world.

Vonnegut begins to emerge as an individual stylist in *Cat's Cradle*. The signature free-flowing, episodic, pop narrative of the book represents a shift away from the conventional plot structures of his earlier novels, with their standard dozen or so chapters, as opposed to *Cat's Cradle's* 127. Scholar James Lundquist attributes some of Vonnegut's lasting popularity, especially among younger readers, to this "structural discontinuity" which he suggests "appeals to an audience accustomed to the montage of television." Vonnegut's short chapters, quick scenes, and pithy dialogue, Lundquist asserts, are the fictional equivalent of watching a TV show, and are thus reflective of "contemporary experience."

A handful of reviewers had kind words for the novel, but for the most part it went the way of his previous books, unnoticed and by and large unbought by the reading public, at first. His next book, *God Bless You, Mr. Rosewater*—a biting satire of middle-class life, in which science-fiction author and Vonnegut alter ego Kilgore Trout makes his first appearance—suffered much the same initial fate.

By 1965, with most of his books out-of-print, the popular magazines folding right and left, and a family to support, Vonnegut needed just about any sort of job and/or break he could get. The University of Iowa provided both when it offered him a two-year faculty position at the school's esteemed Writer's Workshop. He hoped to take the opportunity to begin writing his "Dresden book"—the novel that would eventually become *Slaughterhouse Five*—but found the topic still too difficult to face.

Still, the positive influence of Iowa on Vonnegut's career, as scholar Jerome Klinkowitz notes, is "undebatable." Surrounded by supportive colleagues, the author was encouraged to develop his eccentric style and feel free to refer to himself in his books if he liked, a trademark technique which his earlier publishers had frowned upon. Consequently, many of Vonnegut's post-Iowa novels include autobiographical or semi-autobiographical prologues, in addition, of course, to his sometimes not-so-thinly-disguised portrayals of himself in the texts themselves, e.g. Kilgore Trout, *Player Piano's* Ed Finnerty, the narrator of *Slaughterhouse Five,* et al.

Having lost the market for his short stories, Vonnegut kept his name in the public eye by writing reviews and first-person articles for *The New York Times Book Review, The New York Times Magazine, Esquire,* and others. His reports—many of which were reprinted in *Wampeters, Foma & Granfalloons* (1974)—helped usher in the "New Journalism," a highly personalized, colorful approach to news reporting that, in addition to Vonnegut, was being pioneered by a handful of such writers as Hunter S. Thompson, Tom Wolfe, and Dan Wakefield. Another trick he picked up was to write endorsements, or cover "blurbs" as they are called, for as many books as he could, thus making his name a household word. By the time Vonnegut left Iowa, he found he had gained an audience. His reputation had been slowly spreading, largely by word of mouth, across college campuses and among fans of underground literature nationwide.

Kurt Vonnegut

Publishers began to take notice, as well. In 1966 and 1967, Dell and Avon reissued all of Vonnegut's novels in paperback; in a somewhat futile attempt to put the matter to rest once and for all, the author insisted that the reprints be classified as straight, mass-market paperbacks, instead of science-fiction.

Whether read as science fiction, fantasy, or otherwise, the rise in popularity of Vonnegut's fiction, with its unorthodox plots and unique vocabulary, coincided with the cultural and social revolution that was sweeping the nation during the mid- to late sixties. Young people everywhere were challenging every perceived sacred cow of "the Establishment," from the Vietnam War to punctuation and metered rhyme. Vonnegut was one of many authors whose careers were beginning to peak at about the same time or who were enjoying enduring popularity among young readers, especially at the college-age level. These included such writers as Jack Kerouac, William Burroughs, J. D. Salinger, Herman Hesse, Richard Brautigan, John Barth, Donald Barthelme, and Thomas Pynchon—all highly individualized stylists who defied convention in one way or another, thus capturing the soul of the sixties counterculture.

While many high-minded critics of the day, watching this destruction of American arts and letters from their ivory towers, were bemoaning the so-called "death of the novel," Vonnegut was actually helping to breathe life into a new genre—modern, pop fiction, which by its nature was more culturally in tune with late twentieth-century life than the comparatively inaccessible "literary" classics of the "Proust-Mann-Joyce tradition," as Lundquist (paraphrasing critic Leslie Fiedler) so keenly put it:

> *Vonnegut is thus a transitional figure in a time when the anti-egalitarian values of such earlier figures as T. S. Eliot, who believed that culture is the property of the tiny remnant that can appreciate highly abstruse and allusive symbolic forms of art, are being left behind. Pop, which had been seen as a vice of the populace, is now regarded as a fantastic and fantastically valuable storehouse of dreams, longings and ancient myths retooled.*

Vonnegut's attacks on modern society were misinterpreted as revolutionary, rather than recognized as sardonic eulogies for the middle-class decency and respect he learned from his parents. He was no radical: "[E]verything I believe I was taught in junior civics during the Great Depression" he told *Playboy* magazine in 1973. "I still believe in it. I got a very good grade."

In that interview, conducted towards the end of America's long and devastating involvement in the Vietnam War, Vonnegut also reiterated his antiwar convictions, and expressed pride in the fact that he grew up in a pacifist nation where "the generals had nothing to say about what was done in Washington."

Vonnegut, the veteran, had seen enough of what men at war were capable of at Dresden. In 1967, he received a Guggenheim Fellowship, which allowed him to travel to Europe and research his "Dresden book." Two years later, he finally published the novel which had haunted him for over twenty years—*Slaughterhouse Five*.

True to form, Vonnegut steps forward to directly address the reader in the first and last chapters of the book, which really read like a prologue and epilogue, as well as at various moments here and there throughout the narrative (e.g. "That was I. That was me. That was the author of this book."). Another of Vonnegut's trademark techniques is to dredge up characters from previous books, and thus in the pages of *Slaughterhouse Five* we reencounter Kilgore Trout, Eliot Rosewater, *Cat's Cradle's* Rumfoord and *Sirens'* Tralfamadorians.

Slaughterhouse Five tells the story of Billy Pilgrim, a young chaplain's assistant who survives the bombing of Dresden and returns from World War II to Ilium, New York. On his wedding day, he is kidnapped by aliens, the Tralfamadorians, who share with him their unique concept of time and their determinist philosophy. Human beings, the Tralfamadorians observe, are the only creatures in the universe to speak of "free will." There is no such thing, they say, and existence is simply a series of moments good and bad, which can be experienced over and over again. The often repeated Tralfamadorian saying, "So it goes," which permeates the book, best captures their belief in the inevitability of events, no matter how dire or destructive.

Vonnegut, however, is unwilling to accept this answer "to the disturbing . . . question . . . of why man destroys and kills," scholar Stanley Schatt observed. Vonnegut is "not content to excuse the fire-bombing of Dresden or the Vietnam War as a fate beyond the control of human will," Schatt concludes.

In the end, however, Billy/Vonnegut is able to come to terms with the horror of Dresden by merging the Tralfamadorian's recognition that there is nothing that can be done about death ("So it goes.") with human compassion and hope.

With the publication of *Slaughterhouse Five*, Vonnegut finally achieved the long-awaited recognition he deserved. Reviewers compared him to George Orwell and crowned him America's foremost "black humorist . . . disposed to deep and comic reflection on the human dilemma."[*] All of his books were back in print, several in hardcover, and were selling—only now in college bookstores instead of bus station news-stands—plus his new publisher, Delacorte Press, collected many of his early short stories in *Welcome to the Monkey House* (1969). In 1970, Vonnegut moved to Cambridge, Massachusetts to teach creative writing at Harvard University; the following year the University of Chicago, having accepted *Cat's Cradle* as a thesis, awarded him his previously-denied Master's Degree in anthropology. His first play, *Happy Birthday, Wanda June* (1970), had a five month run on Broadway and National Educational Television hired him to write *Between Time and Timbuktu*, a teleplay collage of scenes from his various books which aired in March of 1972. That same year *Slaughterhouse Five* was produced as a major motion picture. He had, as they say, arrived.

In the midst of all this professional good fortune, Vonnegut's personal life was rapidly unraveling. With his children now

---

[*]By "black humorist," the critics meant that Vonnegut's writing was characteristic of the grim, distorted, and grotesque brand of satire known as "black comedy" or "black humor"; the term does not mean the comedy of African Americans.

grown and on their own, the Cape Cod house seemed vast and empty. His home life fell completely apart in 1971 after he and his wife separated and eventually divorced. Vonnegut left the Cape and moved into an apartment in New York. In 1972, his son Mark suffered a schizophrenic breakdown on a commune in British Columbia and later wrote about his struggle with mental illness in *The Eden Express.*

Now that Vonnegut had finished his "war book," as he wrote in the opening chapter of *Slaughterhouse Five,* he promised himself that the next one was "going to be fun." True to his word, *Breakfast of Champions* is one of his most darkly comic and freewheeling novels, even though "suicide," he claimed "is at the heart of the book." *Slaughterhouse* and *Breakfast* were at one time one novel, Vonnegut said, "[b]ut they just separated completely. It was like . . . oil and water—they were simply not mixable. So I was able to decant *Slaughterhouse Five,* and what was left was *Breakfast of Champions.*"

Breakfast of Champions was a professionally as well as personally cathartic novel. In the preface, Vonnegut calls the book "my fiftieth birthday present to myself." In the irreverent novel's bittersweet climax, the author liberates himself from the past by releasing his stable of characters: "'I am cleansing and renewing myself for the very different sorts of years to come. Under similar spiritual conditions, Count Tolstoi freed his serfs. Thomas Jefferson freed his slaves. I am going to set at liberty all the literary charaters who have served me so loyally during my writing career.'"

Having shed his old characters, Vonnegut nevertheless returned to one of his favorite themes, anti-utopianism, in his next novel, *Slapstick,* which he called his most autobiographical work to date and likened to "grotesque, situational poetry—like the slapstick film comedies, especially those of Laurel and Hardy, of long ago."

One of *Slapstick*'s major themes, as scholar Stanley Schatt has noted, is the "pervading loneliness of contemporary American culture." In the book's preface, Vonnegut mourned the loss of his family's cultural identity and wrote of how the

Depression stripped him and his siblings of their roots, casting them adrift in a new, homogenous American society—a society forged, in part, by the positive impetus of the New Deal, but subject as well to the dehumanization of an increasingly technological, industrial era.

"[I]t was easy for my brother and sister and me to wander away from Indianapolis," he laments. "And, of all the relatives we left behind, not one could think of a reason why we should come home again. / We didn't belong anywhere in particular any more. We were interchangeable parts in the American machine."

The themes of loneliness and separation in contemporary society continued to dominate Vonnegut's next book, the best-seller *Jailbird,* which examines the economic disparities between corporate America, with its powerful systems and conglomerates, and the average, hard-working, middle-class American citizen. In typical fashion, Vonnegut blends autobiographical and historical fact with fiction in this novel about the narrator's/Vonnegut's involvement with the fictitous RAMJAC Corporation and its eccentric major stockholder, Mrs. Jack Graham, Jr., aka bag lady Mary Kathleen O'Looney.

Ignoring his emancipation proclamation, Vonnegut has resurrected old characters here and there in his more recent novels, such as *Bluebeard* (1987), whose hero, the rascally artist Rabo Karabekian, played a minor role in *Breakfast of Champions*. And Vonnegut continues to twist and mold time and space to suit his purposes in such novels as *Galápagos* (1985), set "[o]ne million years ago, back in 1986 A.D." when "[h]uman beings had much bigger brains . . . than they do today, and so they could be beguiled by mysteries."

Despite Vonnegut's efforts to put the impact of Dresden and the Depression behind him, they remain the two defining episodes of his artistic career, which spans almost fifty years and includes more than a dozen novels together with various collections of short fiction, drama, essays, articles, and speeches. While his antiwar, antiestablishment, anticorporate, and pro-middle-class themes may seem anachronistically linked to the revolutionary heydays of the sixties, the common denominator or "thread," as Stanley Schatt phrased it, "that runs through all of Vonnegut's fiction seems to be . . . his continued preoccupation over the question of man's ability to control his own destiny"—certainly a question with a more timeless and lasting pedigree.

Though some science-fiction fans still claim him for their own, Vonnegut successfully extricated himself from that "file drawer" years ago. This is not to say that he has not devoted considerable time and space to the examination of technology and how it has affected humanity or may in the future. Perhaps his most significant contribution, in fact, to late twentieth-century American literature is his formal acknowledgment of the influence of science and machines in modern life. He has crashed the jealously guarded, ivy-covered gates of college English departments and disproved the condescending notion "that you can't be a serious writer and include technology," as he once growled in an interview (quoted by Jerome Klinkowitz). "Any twentieth-century novel reflecting life as it is lived now must have an awful lot of machinery."

By simply yet persistently noticing technology, as he put it, Vonnegut paved the way for many of his like-minded contemporaries on both sides of the Atlantic. From the very earliest stories and novels, his writing anticipated such works as Ray Bradbury's *Fahrenheit 451*, B. F. Skinner's *Walden II*, Anthony Burgess' *A Clockwork Orange,* Arthur C. Clarke's *2001: A Space Odyssey,* and Micheal Crichton's *Andromeda Strain.* What sets Vonnegut apart from the pure science-fiction genre is that no matter how much technology figures in his books, his focus has remained humanistic. "[H]e is essentially a preacher, a moralist, a man with a message" as writer Tim Hildebrand notes. "Most science-fiction writers concentrate on ideas, not people."

Yet, like his character Eliot Rosewater, Vonnegut nutures a special place in his heart for science fiction writers. In a scene at a literary convention in *God Bless You, Mr. Rosewater,* Eliot speaks not only for himself but for Vonnegut when he addresses a group of science fiction authors and says:

> *You're the only ones with guts enough to really care about the future, who really notice what machines do to us, what wars do to us, what cities do to us, what big, simple ideas do to us, what tremendous misunderstandings, mistakes, accidents and catastrophes do to us. You're the only ones zany enough to agonize over time and distances without limit, over mysteries that will never die, over the fact that we are right now determining whether the space voyage for the next billion years or so is going to be Heaven or Hell.*

Chronology

November 11, 1922	born in Indianapolis, Indiana
1937	the Depression puts Kurt Vonnegut, Sr., out of work; the family is forced to sell their home and move to a more modest residence in the suburbs
1940–43	enrolls at Cornell University as a chemistry major; becomes managing editor of the *Cornell Daily Sun*; enlists in army
1944	mother commits suicide; fights in Battle of the Bulge; is captured by Germans and taken to POW camp in Dresden
1945	witnesses bombing of Dresden; marries Jane Marie Cox upon return to the States; enrolls as a graduate student in anthropology at the University of Chicago; begins covering police beat for the Chicago City News Bureau
1948	leaves Chicago without a degree; takes job as a public relations official at General Electric Corporation's research facility in Schenectady, New York
1950	first story, "Report on the Barnhouse Effect," published in *Collier's*; begins selling stories to other popular magazines

1951	quits job at GE and moves to Cape Cod, Massachusetts, to write full time; a year later publishes first novel, *Player Piano,* based on experiences in Schenectady
1959	*The Sirens of Titan*
1963	*Cat's Cradle*
1965	accepts offer to teach at the University of Iowa's Writer's Workshop; *God Bless You, Mr. Rosewater*
1966–67	novels reissued in paperback by Dell and Avon; becomes "underground" favorite; travels to Europe on a Guggenheim Fellowship to research "Dresden book"
1969	*Slaughterhouse Five*; *Welcome to the Monkey House*
1971	separates from wife and moves to New York; son, Mark, suffers a schizophrenic breakdown and later writes about the experience in *The Eden Express*
1973	*Breakfast of Champions*
1976	*Slapstick*
1979	*Jailbird*; marries photographer Jill Krementz
1985	*Galápagos*
1987	*Bluebeard*
1995	*Timequake*

Further Reading

Vonnegut's Works

The Sirens of Titan (New York: Dell, 1959). Vonnegut's "space opera" about humankind's search for meaning on other planets.

Cat's Cradle (New York: Holt, Rinehart and Winston, 1963). A Doomsday fantasy, replete with atomic scientists, Carribean dictators, false religion, and God.

Slaughterhouse Five (New York: Delacorte/Seymour Làwrence, 1969). Vonnegut's masterpiece which explores the question of free will.

Breakfast of Champions (New York: Delacorte/Seymour Lawrence, 1973). The author's cathartic follow-up to *Slaughterhouse Five*, in which he revists the haunting question of why humans destroy life.

Wampeters, Foma, & Granfalloons (New York: Delacorte/Seymour Lawrence, 1974). Collected nonfiction, including articles, speeches, and the unabridged 1973 *Playboy* interview.

Slapstick (New York: Delacorte/Seymour Lawrence, 1976). Futuristic fantasy about the decline of culture in a mechanized society.

Palm Sunday (New York: Delacorte Press, 1981). Autobiographical collage of essays. Provides candid, personal insight into Vonnegut's delightful character.

Fates Worse Than Death (New York: G.P. Putnam's Sons, 1991). Follow-up volume to *Palm Sunday*.

Books About Vonnegut

Jerome Klinkowitz & John Somer, editors, *The Vonnegut Statement* (New York: Dell Publishing Co. Inc., 1973). A collection of original essays on Vonnegut's life and works. Includes comprehensive bibliography, up to and including *Happy Birthday, Wanda June*.

Kurt Vonnegut

Jerome Klinkowitz and Donald Lawler, editors, *Vonnegut in America: An Introduction to the Life and Work of Kurt Vonnegut* (New York: Delacorte Press/Seymour Lawrence, 1977). More original essays on Vonnegut's life and works, up to and including *Slapstick*. Includes good concise biography, bibliography, chronology, and photographs.

James Baldwin
(1924–1987)

*Author James Baldwin overcame racism and
poverty to establish himself as one of the most
influential writers of his day. Weaned on the
fiery rhetoric of the Pentecostal church and largely
self-taught by reading the classics, Baldwin
developed a prose style noted for its intensity
and grace.*
(National Archives)

*O*n a December day in 1987, African-American author James
Baldwin took a final ride through the streets of New York City's
Harlem, where he had been born and raised. He was escorted
by a procession of over five thousand mourners, including

numerous literary, political, and entertainment figures who had known "Jimmy" personally and admired his genius. Over the years, they had linked arms with him in social protest, laughed and toasted with him, and joined him in intense discussions on the significance and power of the African-American voice in modern literature. Now, they had come to lay their brother to rest.

"Jimmy always made us feel good," said poet and playwright Amiri Baraka (LeRoi Jones), one of several celebrities who paid homage to Baldwin that day from the pulpit of the Cathedral of St. John the Divine. "He always made us know we were dangerously intelligent and as courageous as the will to be free!"

James Baldwin's writing career spanned forty years, during which he produced some twenty books as well as plays, poetry, and dozens of essays. Baptized in the fiery rhetoric of religious fanaticism, yet tempered with the refined elegance of the literary masters, his prose was noted for its intensity and grace. He inherited the flickering torch of modern African-American literature from mentor Richard Wright, kindled it to a bright flame, and eventually lit fires in the hearts of many of his literary descendants such as Amiri Baraka, Maya Angelou, and Toni Morrison.

James Arthur Baldwin, was born in Harlem on August 2, 1924, the eldest of nine children. The identity of his father is unknown, but when he was three his mother, Emma Burdis Jones, married David Baldwin, a factory worker and weekend storefront preacher from the South. A stern and brutal man, David Baldwin offered the young James little more than a name, regular beatings, and cruel ridicule of the boy's physical appearance (Baldwin was small and bug-eyed).

An angry man, much of David Baldwin's bitterness stemmed from his hatred and resentment of white people—or "white devils," as he called them—a legacy that his stepson was "frightened" to later realize he had inherited. This is hardly surprising, considering the oppressive and demoralizing conditions that were an everyday fact of life in Harlem where, as

Baldwin wrote, "incessant and gratuitous humiliation and danger" wore away at one's spirit. He recalls being terrorized as a boy, for no good reason, by white police officers—"occupying soldier[s] in a bitterly hostile country" he called them—who left him "flat on [his] back" in an empty lot after frightening him half to death.

When Baldwin ventured downtown, into the rich "white world," he knew "instinctively" that "none of it" was for him. "Why don't you niggers stay uptown where you belong?" muttered a white cop to the thirteen-year-old Baldwin who was crossing the street on his way to the public library on 42nd Street. The message was clear: stay in your place, don't cross "the man," i.e. the white man, and you might live long enough to perpetuate the endless cycle of poverty, crime and violence into which you were born.

One avenue out of this cauldron was the ministry, and at fourteen Baldwin joined the church of Mount Calvary of the Pentecostal Faith where he became "Brother Baldwin," boy preacher. The church kept him off the streets and out of trouble, although in later years he confessed that his ministry was little more than a "gimmick." Exposure to the highly charged environment of the black Pentecostal movement did leave its mark, however, and "the King James Bible [and] the rhetoric of the store-front church," as Baldwin observed in the biographical essay "Notes of a Native Son" (1955), significantly influenced his style.

This period of Baldwin's life would eventually provide material for his first (and many consider his best) novel, *Go Tell It on the Mountain* (1953), the plays *Blues for Mr. Charlie* (1964) and *The Amen Corner* (1968) and such short stories as "The Outing" (1951). Additionally, the titles of many of his works, such as *One Day, When I Was Lost* (1972) and *The Fire Next Time* (1963), are derived from gospel music or Scripture—"an enduring literary legacy of religious subjects and imagery . . . and high moral seriousness," as scholar Keneth Kinnamon observed.

As the religious life began to lose some of its luster (and caused increased friction at home once the young Brother Baldwin began attracting bigger crowds than his stepfather), Baldwin began focusing more attention on his education and writing. Literature was another escape from the squalor and violence of his homelife, and his mother remembered him as a youth, sitting at the kitchen table with a younger sibling in one hand and a book in the other. A precocious reader, by the age of eight, thanks to the guidance of his public school principal and one teacher in particular, he had read *Uncle Tom's Cabin* and was working his way through the works of Dickens, Robert Louis Stevenson, and Dostoyevski.

His earliest creative efforts—poems, essays, stories and plays—earned him the editorship of his junior high school magazine, *The Douglass Pilot,* and impressed celebrated black poet Countee Cullen, literary adviser to the school's English department. He continued to receive support from his teachers at De Witt Clinton, then a primarily white, Jewish high school in the Bronx. As editor of the school paper, *The Magpie,* Baldwin continued to write stories and worked closely with classmates Richard Avedon (today, a world-renowned photographer) and Emile Capouya (later a publisher and literary editor of *The Nation*).

Drifting further from the church and the authoritarian rule of his stepfather, Baldwin the would-be author began to spend time in New York's legendary and colorful Greenwich Village, a magnet for writers, artists, musicians, and eccentrics. It was here he met Beauford Delaney, a gay, black painter and mentor who introduced him to the blues and jazz recordings of Fats Waller, Bessie Smith, and Ella Fitzgerald—music forbidden under his stepfather's roof. In addition to opening Baldwin's ears, Delaney opened his young pupil's eyes and mind by showing him how "art was a way of celebrating the material world, of transcending it and returning to it something of itself in coherent, meaningful form," as Baldwin biographer James Campbell observed in *Talking at the Gates.*

Another influential event during this period was the publication of *Native Son,* Richard Wright's powerful and unprecedented novel of life in the American ghetto. This raw and unapologetic depiction of the black, urban experience established the legitimacy of modern African-American literature. *Native Son* was an inspiration for Baldwin, who was by then scribbling away at a novel of his own. Wright proved "that a black writer need have no fear of competing with whites on equal terms," as Campbell put it.

Baldwin graduated high school in 1942 with thoughts of attending City College of New York. The need to help put food on the table of his impoverished family scotched those plans, however, and he ended up working a series of menial jobs in New Jersey where he once again encountered racism.

"I learned in New Jersey that to be a Negro meant, precisely, that one was . . . at the mercy of the reflexes the color of one's skin caused in other people," he wrote in "Notes of a Native Son," referring in particular to a violent confrontation in a restaurant where he was refused service because he was black. Narrowly escaping a beating, he realized that he was just as ready to commit murder and concluded that "[t]here is not a Negro alive who does not have this rage in his blood."

After a long illness, Baldwin's stepfather died in August of 1943, on the very day that Emma gave birth to their ninth and last child. Only nineteen years old, James was now head of the family and struggled to make ends meet. There were other emotional difficulties as well: Baldwin could now come to terms with his homosexuality, which he had previously repressed, fearing the backlash of his religious stepfather's intolerance. More significantly, David Baldwin's most enduring legacy to the stepson he never loved was an unfulfilled desire *for* love and acceptance from a father figure, an emotional handicap which haunted James Baldwin all his life and appeared as a theme in many of his books.

The following year, a father figure appeared: Baldwin summoned the courage to knock on the Brooklyn door of his literary idol, Richard Wright, and introduced himself.

"I remember our first meeting very well," wrote Baldwin in his tributary essay "Alas, Poor Richard," which appeared in the collection *Nobody Knows My Name: More Notes of a Native Son* (1961).

> *I was broke, naturally, shabby, hungry, and scared . . . We sat in the living room and Richard brought out a bottle of bourbon and ice and glasses . . . [He] talked to me or, rather, drew me out on the subject of the novel I was working on then. I was so afraid of falling off my chair and so anxious for him to be interested in me, that I told him far more about the novel than I, in fact, knew about it, madly improvising . . . I am sure that Richard realized this, for he seemed to be amused by me. But I think he liked me. I know that I liked him . . .*

Yet, just as his father had renounced him, Baldwin would eventually reject Wright—an oedipal pattern of approval-seeking and betrayal he would repeat with other mentors throughout his life. But at this early point in his career, he needed all the support he could get and was fortunate to have Wright not only read his novel but recommend him for a $500 fellowship from Harper & Brothers. Baldwin was awarded the grant in 1945 and the publishers promised to take a look at his book when it was ready. He hastily produced a finished manuscript, but it was rejected twice.

His first commercial sale, a book review, appeared the following year in the pages of *The Nation;* he began to attract attention with more reviews and articles (most notably "The Harlem Ghetto") on racial issues in *New Leader* and *Commentary,* where his first published short story, "Previous Condition," appeared in 1948.

The story underscores Baldwin's frustration and anger as an African American trying to rise above the stereotypes imposed by a racist society. Peter, an out-of-work black actor, is secretly living in an apartment that a white friend, Jules, rented for him. When the landlady discovers Peter is in the building she throws him out.

"'I can't have no colored people here,'" she tells him, echoing a painful refrain from Baldwin's childhood. "'This is a white neighborhood . . . [w]hy don't you go on uptown, like you belong?'" Peter's response is: "'I can't stand niggers.'"

Like Peter, Baldwin was straddling two societies, black and white, and did not feel at home in either. He needed to escape. He had moved to Greenwich Village to get away from Harlem, but a $1,500 cash award from a Rosenwald Foundation Fellowship enabled him put even more distance between his hopeful present and lowly past. After giving a portion of the money to his mother and indulging in a spending spree, he took what was left and bought a plane ticket to Paris, a city where blacks were respected rather than scorned. He arrived there in November of 1948 with just $40 in his pocket, money which was gone by the end of the second day.

Wright, who had moved to Paris himself two years earlier to escape American racism, came to Baldwin's rescue once more. He located some cheap lodgings for his pupil and paved his introduction to some of the city's most distinguished literati, among them Jean-Paul Sartre and Simone de Beauvoir, as well as other American expatriate writers such as Saul Bellow and Truman Capote. Among the friends Baldwin made on his own was the young Swiss painter Lucien Happersburger who later became his lover.

Two essays which Baldwin wrote during his first years in Paris—"Everybody's Protest Novel" (*Zero*, 1949) and "Many Thousand Gone" (*Partisan Review*, 1951)—"solidified his reputation as a controversial critic of black culture" (as scholar David Van Leer notes) but severed his relationship with Wright.

In "Everybody's Protest Novel," Baldwin iconoclastically attacks his boyhood favorite, *Uncle Tom's Cabin*. He claims that the book, as well as all "protest" fiction, though well-intentioned, is ultimately damaging: "fantasies, connecting nowhere with reality, sentimental . . . trapped and immobilized in the sunlit prison of the American dream." In the essay's concluding paragraphs, Baldwin claims that Bigger Thomas, lead character of Wright's *Native Son*, is "Uncle Tom's descendant," and argues that Bigger's "tragedy" is not that he was "cold or black or hungry" but that he "accepted a theology that denies him life" and "admits the possibility that he is sub-human."

Baldwin's implication that *Native Son*, like *Uncle Tom's Cabin*, was "a very bad novel" stunned Wright, whose sensitivity was well known. Baldwin was surprised at Wright's reaction, having fully expected to be "patted on the head" for his "original point of view," as he recounted in "Alas, Poor Richard." He couldn't believe that Wright thought the purpose of the essay was to "destroy his novel and his reputation": "[I]t had not entered my mind," wrote Baldwin "that either of these *could* be destroyed, and certainly not by me."

Wright eventually calmed down but Baldwin widened the gulf between them again—this time for good—with "Many Thousand Gone," an openly critical review of Wright and *Native Son*. In the essay, Baldwin praises Wright's eloquence but questions his stature as a "representative" of all African Americans, a job too "impossible" to fulfill.

Baldwin maintained that he never meant to hurt his mentor, yet he inevitably made more noise about their estrangement than Wright ever did. In interviews later in his career, Baldwin stressed that his objection to *Native Son* had always been the book's ending, which shifts the focus from black urban life to the role which the American Communist party played *in* black urban life; another complaint was that Bigger Thomas was also the only recognizably African-American character in the book. Whenever defending his admiration for Wright, Baldwin often pointed out that such criticisms did not apply to the posthumously published *Lawd Today*, a novel that Baldwin regarded as Wright's best.

Still, Baldwin had to confess that Wright's work "was a road-block in my road, the sphinx, really, whose riddles I had to answer before I could really become myself." Baldwin found the answers to the riddles during the winter of 1951–52 while holed up in the Swiss chalet of his friend and lover, Lucien

Happersburger. It was there that the author finally completed his first novel, *Go Tell It on the Mountain.*

Loosely based on Baldwin's family life and considered to be his most crafted piece of fiction, *Mountain* is the story of Harlem's John Grimes, who experiences a religious conversion on his fourteenth birthday. Autobiographical in many ways, it describes the soul-searching journey of Grimes, who finally comes to terms with his stepfather's rejection and experiences as a black man.

Baldwin wasted no time in shipping his first-born novel off to his literary agent (Helen Strauss of the William Morris Agency, whom he had met through a friend) and was delighted to learn in March of 1952 that Alfred A. Knopf was interested. Could he revise the book a bit and would he come to New York to meet with them, they wondered?

Elated by the news, but broke as ever, Baldwin immediately started scrounging around for boat fare. He ended up hustling $500 from actor and friend Marlon Brando, who had recently become a hot property after his successful Broadway performance in *A Streetcar Named Desire.*

Baldwin's initial meetings with Knopf were disappointing. The editors wanted him to cut some of "Come-to-Jesus!" passages and change the ending, which in the original manuscript made frank mention of John Grimes' homosexuality. In Baldwin's opinion, Knopf may as well have asked him to "burn the book." Back in Paris, he reluctantly made the changes but remained forever wary of editors.

While awaiting publication of *Mountain,* Baldwin began writing the play *The Amen Corner,* which concerns a storefront preacher, Sister Margaret, who tries to maintain her position in the church while struggling to prevent her rebellious son from following in the footsteps of his irreverent jazz musician father. Strauss advised Baldwin to hold off on the play. She tried to explain to Baldwin (as quoted by biographer W. L. Weatherby in *James Baldwin, Artist on Fire*) that "the American theater was not exactly clamoring for plays on obscure aspects of Negro life, especially one written by a virtually unknown author." She recommended instead that he focus on getting some of his short fiction into the popular magazines—a more prudent move for a budding novelist.

Baldwin went ahead and wrote the play anyway, which was eventually staged by Howard University in 1955 and finally made it to Broadway in 1965. It was characteristically stubborn of him to insist on going ahead with the project against his agent's advice. He refused to be "corralled," he noted in the introduction to *The Amen Corner,* into being "a Negro writer . . . expected to write diminishing versions of *Go Tell It on the Mountain* forever."

Go Tell It on the Mountain was published in the spring of 1953 to critical praise. "A striking first novel . . . beautiful, furious" wrote *New York Times* reviewers who compared Baldwin to National Book Award–winning black novelist, Ralph Ellison, author of *Invisible Man.* Other reviews were just as laudatory and Baldwin proudly sent his first copy, lovingly inscribed, to his mother.

The success of *Mountain* helped Baldwin secure a Guggenheim Fellowship in 1954. He returned to New York, where he began working on his next novel, *Giovanni's Room* (1956). His expanded circle of friends now included other up-and-coming young writers such as William Styron and Jack Kerouac. He spent part of the year at a secluded writer's colony in New Hampshire where his only complaint was that it was "damn near impossible to get a drink."

In 1955 he collected several of his popular essays, including the two Wright pieces and "The Harlem Ghetto," in *Notes of a Native Son,* "an elegant mixture of autobiography and political analysis" in the words of scholar David Van Leer. The title paid homage to two of Baldwin's literary idols, Henry James (who wrote *Notes of a Son and Brother*) and *Native Son* author Wright.

More fellowship money funded Baldwin's return to Paris the following year. Meanwhile, the finished manuscript of *Giovanni's Room* was causing commotion among the editors at Knopf. The story was set in Paris, not Harlem as they had expected, and there was not a single black character in the book. ("Whites want Black writers to mostly deliver something as [if] it were an official version of the Black experience," an unrealistic expectation, Baldwin said years later.)

On top of it all, the novel dealt overtly and quite graphically with homosexuality, a taboo subject for mainstream publishers of the day. Publishing *Giovanni's Room* as it was, the Knopf editors told him, was out of the question: it would alienate his audience and ruin his career. But toning down the sexual passages, in Baldwin's opinion, meant scrapping the book altogether. He went instead to a London publisher who was more than willing to offer him a book contract; later, Dial Press in New York was similarly brave enough to accept the book and became Baldwin's publisher for most of his career.

In September of 1956, Baldwin's attention shifted back to the United States. His political activism was awakened by an arresting news photo of a 15-year-old African-American girl in Charlotte, North Carolina, surrounded by a jeering and violent white mob as she was trying to gain admission to the local school. Just two years earlier, the Supreme Court, in its historic *Brown v. Board of Education* decision, had mandated that America's public schools be integrated "with all deliberate speed." But in the deep South, home at the time to the majority of the nation's segregated classrooms, stubborn school administrators interpreted "all deliberate speed" as "never."[*]

The civil rights movement, however, was gradually gaining momentum. Activist groups were methodically chipping away at the foundations of segregation and discrimination in America with marches and demonstrations throughout the country. These demonstrations were especially explosive in the South, where discrimination had been a cultural norm for generations.

In the fall of 1957, Baldwin paid his first visit there, to report on the race situation for *Harper's*. As his plane "hovered over

---

[*] Ten years after *Brown v. Board of Education,* only 13,000 (less than one half of one percent) of the almost three million African-American students in the South went to integrated schools.

the rust-red earth of Georgia, [he] could not suppress the thought that this earth had acquired its color from the blood that had dripped down" from the bodies of lynched African Americans. He reflected that his "father must have seen such sights" and as he toured several cities (including Atlanta, where he met Martin Luther King), Baldwin felt a spiritual kinship with southern blacks, from whom he was "but one generation removed": the "bitter interracial history" of the South, he observed, was plainly and sorrowfully "written in their faces."

Baldwin played a high-profile, active role in the civil rights movement—lecturing, taking part in demonstrations, organizing a confrontational meeting between prominent blacks and then-Attorney General Robert F. Kennedy,[*] and writing numerous influential articles and essays, some of which were collected in *Nobody Knows My Name: More Notes of a Native Son.*

Baldwin returned to Greenwich Village in the early sixties where he renewed friendships with many writers, poets, and journalists of the "Beat Generation" (see the Kerouac chapter for more on the Beats). As his reputation grew, so, finally, did his bank account. He was generous with his money, helping family members and friends whenever they were in need. He also liked to travel and if he was having a hard time finishing a book or an article, he would fly off to some hideaway—perhaps as nearby as New Hampshire or as distant as Istanbul, Turkey—to avoid the temptations of his active social life and get to work. He often took on more assignments than he could handle, juggling various projects at once, which ultimately meant that he never had enough time for any of them. After six years of false starts and interruptions, however, he finally

---

[*] Baldwin and some of the others at the meeting were outraged at having to plead with their government for their legal rights. Kennedy tried placating them, relating how his Irish immigrant grandparents had once been victims of discrimination in America, and now his brother was President of the United States—it just required patience. "Your family has been here for three generations and your brother's on top," Baldwin (as quoted by Richard Reeves in *President Kennedy: Profile of Power*) replied angrily. "My family has been here a lot longer than that and we're on the bottom. That's the heart of the problem."

completed his third and possibly most ambitious novel, *Another Country* (1962).

This long and complex novel of love and human relationships is set in the familiar landscape of Manhattan. It tells the story of a disconsolate jazz musician during his final days and the reactions of his friends to his suicide.

Critical reception of *Another Country* ran the gamut from "brilliantly . . . told" and "powerful" to "mediocre" and "obscene," sometimes within the same review. Nonetheless, the book was an immediate best-seller, second only to William Golding's popular *Lord of the Flies* when issued in paperback in 1963. That same year Baldwin's face appeared on the cover of *Time* magazine and *Life* ran a nine-page feature story on him. His reputation as a serious writer was now secured and he welcomed the accompanying fame, wealth and scholarly recognition. "If his essays, subtle and discriminating, were his 'cool mode,'" biographer Campbell wrote, "*Another Country* showed Baldwin playing, as jazz musicians say, on top of the beat."

As the country's political turmoil heated up during the mid- to late sixties—with riots, protests and demonstrations for civil rights and against the Vietnam War—so did the level of Baldwin's involvement, in person, as a public speaker, and in his writing.[*] His play, *Blues for Mister Charlie* (1964), based on the true story of Emmett Till, a Northern black youth murdered in Mississippi for supposedly whistling at a white woman, was noted (and condemned) for the volume of anger it directed at southern bigots. More restrained, but no less powerful, *The Fire Next Time*, released a year earlier, remains one of the most eloquent statements on racial injustice published during this period.

This slim volume consists of two previously published pieces: "My Dungeon Shook: Letter to My Nephew on the One Hundredth Anniversary of the Emancipation" and "Letter from a Region in My Mind." "My Dungeon Shook,"

---

* Baldwin's politics and open homosexuality prompted the notoriously anti-leftist, homophobic Federal Bureau of Investigation to compile a lengthy dossier on his activities.

James Baldwin

An outspoken civil-rights activist, Baldwin issued perhaps his most powerful and impassioned political warning in the pages of The Fire Next Time. *Pictured here at a press conference the day after the assassination of black nationalist leader Malcom X, Baldwin warned that "[w]hat happened to him will probably happen to all of us. The climate that you have created in the West puts everyone's life in danger."*
(Library of Congress)

originallypublished in *The Progressive*, is a brief essay which argues that black freedom depended, as Martin Luther King had preached, upon liberating whites from their racial hatred by accepting them with love. "Letter from a Region in My Mind" (a *New Yorker* article retitled "Down at the Cross" in the book) is a lengthier piece which recounts Baldwin's early ministerial career and rejection of Christianity, a sympathetic report on the Nation of Islam, and a political and historical analysis of racism in the United States. In the book's final passages, Baldwin reiterates the thesis of the first essay while emphasizing his racial pride and adding some strong words of warning:

> [W]e, the black and the white, deeply need each other here if we are really to become a nation—if we are really, that is, to achieve our identity, our maturity, as men and women . . . It is entirely unacceptable that I should have no voice in the political affairs of my own country, for I am not a ward of America; I am one of the first Americans to arrive on these shores . . . If we . . . do not falter in our duty now, we may be able, handful that we are, to end the racial nightmare . . . and change the history of the world. If we do not now dare everything, the fulfillment of that prophecy, re-created from the Bible in song by a slave, is upon us: God gave Noah the rainbow sign, No more water, the fire next time!

By the end of the decade, however, Baldwin had lost some of *his* fire. The upheaval and violence of the times had left him, and the rest of the nation, stunned. He was tired of the funerals—funerals for the freedom riders, the four young black girls killed in an Alabama church bombing, Emmett Till, the NAACP's Medgar Evers, Malcolm X, Martin Luther King, Robert Kennedy.

Disillusioned and overworked, he started to lose his freshness and "exhibited the symptoms of the writer who is losing faith in his material," noted Campbell. His only book in 1965 was *Going to Meet the Man*, a collection of short stories, most of which were previously published. As America's preeminent black author, he also found himself under attack from all sides of the black literary community. He was too radical for traditionalists such as Langston Hughes, but not radical enough for militant blacks such as Leroi Jones (Amiri Baraka).

Baldwin's habitual solution when stuck in a personal and professional rut was a change of scenery. He retreated to Istanbul, Turkey and began work on his next novel, the critical flop *Tell Me How Long the Train's Been Gone* (1968)—a structureless, plotless story about militant, black nationalism. He recaptured some of the power of his earlier prose in his next book, *No Name in the Street* (1972), a memoir of the sixties centered around the life and death of Martin Luther King. During this time he was also under contract with Columbia Pictures to write a screenplay of Alex Haley's *The Autobiography of Malcolm X* but abandoned the project after struggling with studio executives for artistic control.[*]

While in Istanbul, Baldwin was hospitalized for hepatitis. His doctors advised him to give up cigarettes and alcohol, but Baldwin, a lover of high living, ignored them. Soon after, in Paris, he fell seriously ill once more and went to a fashionable seaside resort, St. Paul-de-Vence, in the south of France, to convalesce. He loved the locale so much that he eventually bought an old estate there and made it his home base.

Returning to his roots, Baldwin set his next novel, *If Beale Street Could Talk* (1974), in the streets of Harlem. The main characters, Tish and Fonny, are young black lovers, poised at the threshold of their future together. The hostility of their urban environment crashes down on them, however, leaving their fate uncertain. While praised as a "moving" and "vividly human" novel, *Beale Street* has some glaring narrative problems. Tish tells the story in the first third of the book, but then Baldwin shifts to third person and uses his voice—with all its sophisticated, rhetorical flares—while retaining Tish as narrator. This results in some fairly implausible passages, where Tish, for example, might use lofty language to ponder the

---

*The screenplay was eventually published under the title *One Day, When I Was Lost*.

nature of "truth" or the male ego and then lapse back into black English a few sentences later. Tish, as narrator, also relates scenes, incidents and conversations to which she was not a firsthand witness, such as Fonny's experiences in prison or her mother's trip to Puerto Rico. Instead of crafting the plot to allow for Tish to somehow logically recount these details, Baldwin awkwardly intercedes with his authorial voice: "Joseph and Frank, as we learn later, have also been sitting in a bar, and this is what happened between them." Despite some powerful prose and memorable scenes, *Beale Street* "does not fulfill its artistic potential," according to scholar Kinnamon.

The late seventies and early eighties were years of steady production for Baldwin. He continued to attack racism and discrimination in America wherever he saw it: in Hollywood, for instance, in such films as *Lawrence of Arabia* (an "updated . . . version of Rudyard Kipling's *Gunga Din*") and others which he describes from his point of view in *The Devil Finds Work* (1976). Bigotry and homophobia remained themes in his final novel, *Just Above My Head* (1979) in which the black characters reject white society and turn instead to their own community and culture for salvation.

He returned to the Unites States in 1983 to accept a part-time professorship at the University of Massachusetts at Amherst, where he was invited to lecture on creative writing and civil rights. In 1986, France bestowed on him the prestigious Légion d'Honneur. He had come a long, long way from the impoverished streets of Harlem and the cheap hotel on Paris' Left Bank.

Although he suffered two heart attacks in his late fifties, Baldwin seriously believed that, like Martin and Malcolm before him, an assassin's bullet would take his life. His assassin, however, turned out to be cancer. By 1987, he was confined to his bed in the old farmhouse he bought in St. Paul-de-Vence, where his youngest brother, David, and his old friend Lucien cared for him until his death on November 30.

James Baldwin was one of the "big three" authors of post–World War II African-American literature. Together with Richard Wright and Ralph Ellison, he helped pave the way for and influenced the works of other esteemed black writers such as Toni Morrison, Alice Walker, Paule Marshall, and Amiri Baraka as well as some white writers, like William Styron.

Towards the end of Baldwin's life, some critics took issue with what they saw as a conflict between his art and his activism, between Baldwin the writer and Baldwin the public symbol of racial pride. They accused him of flogging away at the same issues over and over again—race, sexual preference, religious, and familial tensions. But, as scholar Van Leer noted, Baldwin's significance during his early years lay in "his realistic depiction of the psychological effects of racism within the black community." His exploration of this environment in his fiction, nonfiction, and drama naturally led to an expanded analysis of oppression in general—sexual, racial, and otherwise—because he had courageously confronted oppression all his life.

"[A] writer has to take all the risks of putting down what he sees," Baldwin once said. The price he paid for bearing witness to the social ills of his generation was high: self-exile, public ridicule, critical scorn. Yet James Baldwin was never ashamed of anything he wrote or said. He spoke the truth, as he saw it, without apology. "[A]ttacked or not, repressed or not, suddenly newsworthy or not," said Amiri Baraka on the day of Baldwin's funeral, "Jimmy did what Jimmy was."

Chronology

August 2, 1924	born in New York City
1938–42	as a teen, preaches at church of Mount Calvary of the Pentecostal Faith; attends De Witt Clinton High School in the Bronx and serves as editor of school paper; graduates class of '42 with plans to attend City College of New York, but is forced to take series of menial jobs in New Jersey to support family after stepfather dies a year later
1944	befriends Richard Wright
1948	first short story, "Previous Condition," appears in *Commentary;* joins Wright in Paris; eventually offends Wright and ends their friendship by criticizing him in essays "Everybody's Protest Novel" (1949) and "Many Thousand Gone" (1951)
1953	first novel, *Go Tell It on the Mountain,* a critical triumph
1954–56	receives Guggenheim Fellowship; returns to U.S.; publishes collection of essays *Notes of a Native Son* (1955) followed by controversial second novel, *Giovanni's Room* (1956)
1957	first trip to the South to report on racial tension and civil rights movement

James Baldwin

1962	*Another Country*
1963	*The Fire Next Time*
1974	*If Beale Street Could Talk*
November 30, 1987	dies at his villa in St. Paul-de-Vence, France

Further Reading

Baldwin's Works

Go Tell It on the Mountain (New York: Alfred A. Knopf, 1953). Baldwin's powerful first novel.

Notes of a Native Son (Boston: Beacon Press, 1955). A collection of some of Baldwin's early essays.

Nobody Knows My Name: More Notes of a Native Son (New York: Dial Press, 1961). Contains some of Baldwin's best essays on racism and civil rights.

Another Country (New York: Dial Press, 1962). Love, death, and racial tension in New York City during the fifties.

The Fire Next Time (New York: Dial Press, 1963). Powerful statement on racial injustice in the United States.

The Amen Corner (New York: Dial Press, 1968). Baldwin's first play, inspired by his days as a storefront preacher.

Going to Meet the Man (New York: Dial Press, 1965). Collection of short fiction.

If Beale Street Could Talk (New York: Dial Press, 1974). Two lovers, beset by poverty and injustice, struggle to remain united.

Books About Baldwin

James Campbell, *Talking at the Gates: A Life of James Baldwin* (New York: Viking, 1991). A good, comprehensive, adult, easy-to-read biography; includes bibliography.

David Leeming, *James Baldwin* (New York: Alfred A. Knopf, 1994). Most recent biography, written by Baldwin's former secretary; includes chronological bibliography, index.

Horace A. Porter, *Stealing the Fire: The Art and Protest of James Baldwin* (Middletown, CT: Wesleyan University Press, 1989). Insightful and thorough study of Baldwin's works in biographical context. Chronology and extensive bibliography.

Valerie Smith, Lea Baechler, and A. Walton Litz, editors, *African American Writers* (New York: Collier Books, Macmillan Publishing, 1993). Concise, critical biographies of various African-American authors from the 1700s to the present, including Baldwin, Wright, Ellison, Baraka, Morrison, Walker, and others. Excellent resource for broad overview of major African-American literary figures.

Flannery O'Connor
(1925–1964)

*Devoutly Catholic, Flannery O'Connor viewed
existence as a deeply spiritual struggle
between temptation and moral behavior. She
nevertheless had a very dry sense of humor
which imbues her often disturbing stories with a
very bizarre and comic irony.*
(Flannery O'Connor Collection, Ina Dillard Russell
Library, Georgia College)

*I*n 1931, a New York newsreel company, the Pathé News,
dispatched a cameraman to Savannah, Georgia, to record the
ambulatory antics of a chicken with the unique ability to walk
backwards. This bizarre behavior delighted the bird's owner,
five-year-old Flannery O'Connor, who says she subsequently

developed a "passion" for collecting birds, especially those that were odd or deformed. "I wanted one with three legs or three wings but nothing in that line turned up," she later confessed.

O'Connor kept her fondness for pet fowl throughout her life; she also never lost her eye for the unusual, and liberally populated her fiction with various "grotesque" characters whose deformities, she believed, offered insights into the human condition.

"Whenever I am asked why Southern writers particularly have a penchant for writing about freaks, I say it is because we are still able to recognize one," she reasoned in her 1965 essay "Some Aspects of the Grotesque in Southern Fiction." "To be able to recognize a freak, you have to have some conception of the whole man, and in the South the general conception of man is still, in the main, theological."

So too was O'Connor's vision of life, which she viewed as an ongoing "conflict between an attraction for the Holy and the disbelief in it that we breathe in the air of the times."

Mary Flannery O'Connor was born on March 25, 1925, in Savannah, Georgia, the only child of Regina (Cline) and Edward Francis O'Connor, Jr. Her ancestors on both sides of the family had emigrated from Ireland in the mid-nineteenth century and were among Georgia's earliest Irish Catholic settlers. O'Connor's maternal grandfather, Peter James Cline, prospered as a merchant during the Civil War and became the first Catholic mayor of Milledgeville, Georgia, the town where Regina was born and Flannery eventually spent most of her life.

As a member of Georgia's minority population of Catholics, O'Connor grew up feeling "both native and alien" in the heavily Protestant southern society. Still, she believed that the South was "good ground for Catholic fiction"—an environment which, if no longer Christ-centered, was "most certainly Christ-haunted," as she noted in her 1963 lecture "The Catholic Novelist in the South."[*] There were also advantages, she ob-

---

[*] Published posthumously in *Viewpoint*, Spring 1966; also in Flannery O'Connor, *Mystery and Manners; Occasional Prose*, edited by Sally and Robert Fitzgerald, as well as in O'Connor's *Collected Works*, selected by Sally Fitzgerald. (See bibliography.)

served, to living in a culture where even the most ignorant and uneducated had some familiarity with the Bible: "The writer whose themes are religious particularly needs a region where these themes find a response in the life of the people, and this condition is met in the South as nowhere else."

Young Mary Flannery (she didn't drop the "Mary" from her name until after college) attended parochial school, where she enjoyed writing and drawing; summers were spent in Milledgeville at her mother's family house in the teeming company of various aunts, uncles, and cousins. O'Connor's father, a real estate dealer, had his own business but, like most Americans, was hard hit by the Depression. It was also around this time that he began to suffer from an illness, initially diagnosed as arthritis, which turned out to be lupus erythematosus, an incurable disease which causes the body's immune system to attack its own vital tissue.

In 1938, the O'Connors moved to Atlanta where Flannery's father Edward took a job with the Federal Housing Administration (FHA). The relocation proved too stressful for his family, however, so he moved into a boarding house by himself while Regina and Mary Flannery went to live in the Cline home in Milledgeville. Edward visited them there on weekends.

Mary Flannery set up a studio for herself in the attic where she continued to draw and write stories, producing cartoons and articles for her high school paper. She also drew attention to herself in her home economics class by sewing clothing ("a white piqué coat with a lace collar and two buttons in the back") for one of her chickens. Among her favorite authors was Edgar Allan Poe, whose *Narrative of Arthur Gordon Pym* and collection of humorous stories inspired her to become a writer.

By 1940, Edward O'Connor's illness forced him to resign his FHA job and retire to Milledgeville, where he died in February of the following year. Young Mary Flannery deeply felt the loss and rarely spoke of her father ever again.

O'Connor graduated from high school in 1942 (in her yearbook she listed "collecting rejection slips" as one of her hobbies) and enrolled in the summer-school freshman class of the Georgia State College for Women (now Georgia College) as a dual sociology and English major. Aside from her avoidance of dances and sports, she was fairly active in student affairs, serving as art editor of the newspaper, feature editor of the yearbook, and regularly contributed fiction to the school's literary quarterly, *The Corinthian.*

In her junior year, she sent some of her cartoons to *The New Yorker* which rejected them, but at least included some words of encouragement; she had no luck selling fiction to commercial publications either. One of her English teachers, however, was impressed enough with her work to bring her to the attention of the graduate writing program at the University of Iowa, more popularly known as the Writer's Workshop. The school offered O'Connor a scholarship, and upon graduation from Georgia in June of 1945 the budding author moved to Iowa City, where she wrote to her mother every day and kept up on local happenings by reading the Milledgeville newspaper.

Iowa significantly broadened O'Connor's intellectual horizons. Workshop director Paul Engle introduced her to the works of James Joyce, Franz Kafka, William Faulkner, and other moderns and encouraged her to submit her work to literary magazines. A subsequent director, Paul Hogan, advised her to write for a set number of uninterrupted hours at the same time each day, a work schedule she would adhere to for the rest of her career. In March of 1946, one of her stories, "The Geranium," was finally accepted by a literary magazine, *Accent,* which published the piece in its summer issue under the name she now preferred to use, Flannery O'Connor. She began to work on a novel and won a Rinehart-Iowa Fiction Award for the first four chapters; the prize included $750 and a publishing option by Rinehart.

O'Connor returned to Iowa for postgraduate studies after receiving her master of fine arts degree in June of 1947. She continued to work on her novel, selling bits and pieces of it in story form to various publications like *Sewanee Review* and *Partisan Review.* In the spring of 1948, she accepted an invitation from the Yaddo Foundation to spend June and July at its renowned artist's colony in Saratoga Springs, New York. There she befriended various members of the literati such as poet (and famed Catholic convert) Robert Lowell and poet/critic/editor Malcolm Cowley.

O'Connor stayed at Yaddo through the summer and into the fall, having declined the offer of an Iowa fellowship, and forged ahead with her book, which she brought to the favorable attention of literary agent Elizabeth McKee. McKee sent nine chapters of the novel to John Selby at Rinehart, whose critical comments infuriated O'Connor.

"The letter is addressed to a slightly dim-witted Camp-fire Girl, and I cannot look with composure on getting a lifetime of others like them," she wrote to McKee from Saratoga in February of 1949. O'Connor's letter to Selby, in which she stressed that she was "not writing a conventional novel," was less inflammatory but concluded with this spirited shot across the bow: "I am amenable to criticism but only within the sphere of what I am trying to do; I will not be persuaded to do otherwise. The finished book . . . will be just as odd if not odder than the nine chapters you have now. The question is: is Rinehart interested in publishing this kind of novel?"

The ultimate answer was no, it was not, and a year later the publisher released its option on O'Connor's book. In the meantime, a political scandal at Yaddo (an FBI investigation targeted one of the former residents, journalist Agnes Smedley, as a Soviet spy and Yaddo director Elizabeth Ames as a Communist sympathizer) had forced the residents to leave and O'Connor went to New York with Lowell, who introduced her to various members of New York's literary circle such as editor Robert Giroux of Harcourt, Brace and Company. O'Connor also became a close friend of poet/translator Robert Fitzgerald and his wife Sally—so close, in fact, that she went to live with the Fitzgeralds in Ridgefield, Connecticut, where she wrote in the mornings and baby-sat for the couple's eldest child in the afternoons. She spent her evenings engaged in long, after-dinner discussions about literature, religion, and stories from "down home."

In the fall of 1949, she received a letter of interest in her book from Harcourt Brace. This happy news was overshadowed by the onset of what appeared to be arthritis, which flared up while she was back home in Georgia over Christmas. She was hospitalized and returned to Connecticut in the spring, but her condition worsened. Finally, an Atlanta doctor diagnosed disseminated lupus erythematosus, the same fatal illness which killed her father. O'Connor came dangerously close to death that year but was saved by blood transfusions and massive injections of a new experimental cortisone derivative, ACTH.

Upon her release from the hospital in March of 1951, O'Connor moved into her mother's new home, a 1,500-acre farm four miles outside of Milledgeville. The property had been left to Regina O'Connor by an uncle and was called Andalusia. Too weak to climb stairs (the ACTH had weakened her bones to the point where her hips could no longer bear her weight), O'Connor took a room on the ground floor and worked on revising her novel, now titled *Wise Blood* (1952), which Harcourt, Brace had accepted in October of 1950.

Labeled a "tragicomedy" by some, *Wise Blood* is the story of Hazel Motes, the disillusioned young grandson of a preacher, just out of the army and heading back home to Eastrod, Tennessee.

Critical reaction to *Wise Blood* was mixed. *Newsweek* went so far as to declare that O'Connor was "perhaps the most gifted of the youngest generation of American novelists," but reviewers by and large were either confused or repelled by the book, with its grotesque cast of characters and grim ending. Local response to the novel was mixed as well: many Milledgeville residents were proud to have a published author in their midst, but those who actually read the book were outraged. Scholar Kathleen Feeley describes how the town responded to O'Connor's notoriety "with characteristic Southern graciousness" by hosting several autograph parties, during which O'Connor spent most of the time silently scowling in a corner. "They

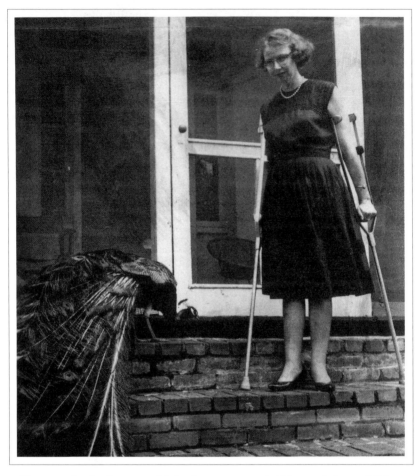

Bone-weakening hormonal injections to control O'Connor's lupus left her handicapped for much of her adult life. Still, she remained energetic enough to go on lecture tours or tend to her favorite birds—peacocks—on her mother's 1,500-acre farm, Andalusia, outside Milledgeville, Georgia.
(Library of Congress)

never had another one," Feeley quotes O'Connor's mother as recalling years later.

In 1953, O'Connor was awarded a $2,000 *Kenyon Review* fellowship, which she wryly surmised would cover the costs of her blood transfusions and drug treatments. She continued to write in the mornings and in the afternoons read, painted, or tended to her herds of peacocks. These resplendent creatures were her favorites and she often judged individuals by their reactions to the birds: "Many people, I have found, are congenitally unable to appreciate the sight of a peacock. Once or twice I have been asked what the peacock is 'good for'—a question which gets no answer from me because it deserves none."

O'Connor referred to her next book, a collection of short fiction entitled *A Good Man Is Hard to Find* (1955), as "stories of original sin." The volume contains several of her masterpieces, including the title piece, "Good Country People," "The Life You Save May Be Your Own," and "The Artificial Nigger," which happened to be her personal favorite. Set in disturbingly bleak rural landscapes, the conflict of many of these stories usually pivots on the interactions of three prototypical O'Connor characters: the well-intentioned, but morally overbearing care-giver, the deformed dependent, and the morally corrupt, sometimes violent drifter who shatters the dependent-care-giver relationship.

Another recurring element of O'Connor's fiction, readily evident in *A Good Man Is Hard to Find,* is what she termed the "moment of grace" or epiphany—"some gesture of a character that is unlike any other in the story," one that is "both in character and beyond character," as she once put it in one of her college lectures. At such a moment, O'Connor suggested, the character touches "both the world and eternity" and "somehow [makes] contact with mystery."

One memorable "moment of grace" takes place in "A Good Man Is Hard to Find," when the self-righteous grandmother feels compassion for The Misfit—one of the escaped convicts who ends up killing her and her family on a deserted country road. In that moment she recognizes the bond of humanity that exists between them and goes so far as to call him one of her children.

In "Good Country People," a woman impatiently endures the annoying prattle and platitudes of her mother and the house boarder while secretly longing for love. She plans to seduce the traveling Bible salesman, Manley Pointer, but is instead conned by the young man. Being "good country people," he tells her, "ain't held me back none." He convinces her to let him see and remove her artificial leg, which "she was as sensitive about . . . as a peacock about his tail," then steals it and her glasses, and leaves her, helpless, in a hayloft, thus destroying "her illusions and her defenses," as scholar Dorothy Tuck MacFarland observed. Yet the woman's moment of vulnerability may be the key to her "salvation." From the barn loft window, she watches the salesman crossing the pasture, which to her blurred vision appears to be a "green speckled lake," suggesting the image of Christ walking on the water.

Allusions to Christ appear once again in "The Artificial Nigger" when the country grandfather, Mr. Head, denies knowledge of his grandson, Nelson (Peter's denial of Christ) after the boy has gotten into trouble on their day trip to the big city. The pair are reunited, however, before the "plaster figure of a Negro" perched on a wall, "as if they were faced with some great mystery, some monument to another's victory"—Christ's crucifixion—"that brought them together in their common defeat."

The dramatization of moral conflict is, as scholar Preston M. Browning, Jr. observed, at "the gravitational center of [O'Connor's] . . . artistic vision." While virtually an invalid on a backwoods farm in Georgia, this southern author was by no means a simple, yarn-spinning yokel. She was a voracious reader of philosophy and a deep thinker who, as Browning notes, was occupied with "the primary spiritual question of our era," i.e. the search for meaning and the erosion of faith.

"My audience," O'Connor once confided to a friend, "are the people who think God is dead"—a philosophical debate with roots in eighteenth- and nineteenth-century Western thought and which the media was helping to broadcast by the twentieth century of O'Connor's day.[*]

---

[*]In 1966, the question of God's demise—"Is God Dead?"—was posed by *Time* magazine in one of the most famous cover stories in the history of journalism.

Without question, O'Connor was a "theological writer," an appellation which the London *Times* bestowed upon her and which she cherished. "I have found . . . from reading my own writing" she once noted, "that my subject in fiction is the action of grace in territory held largely by the devil." To her, the questioning of God's grace or of His existence are the sins that lead her characters down the path of "self-deception" and thereby to evil.

"If [Jesus] did what He said, then it's nothing for you to do but throw away everything and follow Him," concludes The Misfit, just before he murders the grandmother. "[A]nd if He didn't, then it's nothing for you to do but to enjoy the few minutes you got left the best way you can—by killing somebody or burning down his house or doing some other meanness to him."

O'Connor explores this territory again in her second novel, *The Violent Bear It Away* (1960). In the novel, the protagonist, a young man educated by his Bible-thumping uncle, comes to doubt his relative's righteousness and questions his own belief in God. As in O'Connor's other works, violence permeates the novel, forcing into stark relief concepts of sin and its by-product, redemption.

Many critics and readers have been disturbed by the amount of violence permeating O'Connor's fiction—violence which is often savage and unexpected, as in "A Good Man Is Hard to Find." Yet such brutality is necessary, O'Connor once commented, if her characters are ever to be redeemed: "I have found that violence is strangely capable of returning my characters to reality and preparing them for their moment of grace. Their heads are so hard that almost nothing else will do the work." Viewed in the larger context of her religious beliefs, the spiritual life itself is one of violent struggles—between faith and reason, morality and immorality, humility and pride.

Like *Wise Blood, The Violent Bear It Away* received mixed reviews. O'Connor complained that the critics, both favorable and negative, misunderstood her intentions. The attention, however, nudged her a little further into the limelight and interviewers began showing up at Andalusia with increasing frequency while lecture invitations from all over the United States started rolling in.

O'Connor endured her celebrity with characteristic wryness. She told one interviewer that the reason she liked "to publish short stories is that nobody pays attention to them . . . When you publish a novel, the racket is like a fox in a hen house." When asked, during one of her college lectures, by a student whose voice was "loaded with cunning: 'Miss O'Connor, what is the significance of The Misfit's hat?'" she paused for a moment and replied, "Its significance is to cover his head." One of her most famous rejoinders was in response to the stock question, "Why do you write?" Her answer: "Because I am good at it." The literary establishment agreed. Between 1953 and 1964 she received several O. Henry Awards, grants from the National Institute of Arts and Letters and the Ford Foundation, plus honorary degrees from the University of Notre Dame and Smith College.

Physically, however, O'Connor continued to suffer complications from her disease and its treatment. By 1956, she was told that she would have to use crutches for the rest of her life due to the extensive deterioration of her hip caused by her medications. In 1958, she took a trip to Europe that included an audience in Rome with Pope Pius XII and a pilgrimage to Lourdes, where she reluctantly bathed in waters from the sacred spring, praying for the success of her books instead of her health. Six months later, her hip unexpectedly improved and she was able to walk without crutches, attributing the recovery to the miraculous waters at Lourdes. More symptoms soon developed, however—anemia, pain in her jaws, renewed pain in her hips. Novocain provided temporary relief and doctors investigated various surgical procedures, such as steel hip joints or the use of bone grafts, but the possibility of destabilizing O'Connor's lupus made such operations too risky.

In February of 1964, O'Connor's doctor diagnosed a tumor as the cause of her anemia and scheduled her for an operation, despite the risks involved. Even though she was given massive doses of cortisone as a preventive measure and the tumor was successfully removed, the lupus was reactivated and she spent the spring in and out of the hospital. She retained her high spirits through it all, hiding half-written stories under her pillow, fearing that the nurses would forbid her to work. Responding to a letter from an English teacher, she wrote: "I'm sorry I can't answer [your note] more fully but I am in the hospital and am not up to literary questions . . . As for Mrs. May, I must have named her that because I knew some English teacher would write and ask me why. I think you folks sometimes strain the soup too thin . . ."

During these convalescent months, O'Connor kept working, preparing what would be her final collection of short stories, *Everything That Rises Must Converge* (1965). Seven of the nine stories in the book were previously published; the concluding tale, "Judgment Day," was, ironically, a reworking of her very first published story, "The Geranium."

O'Connor took her title from the writings of a Jesuit paleon-tologist-philosopher, Pierre Teilhard de Chardin. In his book *The Phenomenon of Man*, Teilhard hypothesized that evolution is an ongoing progression towards higher levels of consciousness, culminating in a mental and spiritual union with God Himself. As various species continue to "rise," or evolve into higher forms of conscious awareness, like the lines of a globe radiating outward and upward, they ultimately combine or "converge" upon one another at what Teilhard called the "Omega point," which is total Being, or God. This hypothesis places the emergence of *Homo sapiens*, man, somewhere around the middle of the globe, rather than at its peak, as some believe.

The stories in the collection—including the title story, "The Enduring Chill," "Greenleaf," "The Comforts of Home," and "The Lame Shall Enter First"—follow the same thematic pattern, in which the protagonist, as MacFarland notes, is brought "to a vision of himself as he really is," thus making "possible a true rising toward Being." While corresponding to the teachings of Teilhard, this dynamic, as Browning observed, also reflects a larger, fundamental Christian belief—repeated over and over in O'Connor's fiction—in "man's ability to be radically altered by grace."

O'Connor did not live to see the publication of *Everything That Rises Must Converge.* Several weeks after returning to Andalusia from the hospital on June 20, she called for a priest so that she could receive the Sacrament of the Sick. She continued to work for a couple of hours each morning, revising the text of "Judgment Day," but by the end of July became exhausted and was admitted to Baldwin County Hospital. On August 2 she slipped into a coma and died of kidney failure the following day, August 3, 1964. She was 39 years old. She was buried beside her father the next day, following a Requiem Mass at the Sacred Heart Church in Milledgeville.

Despite the brevity of Flannery O'Connor's career, her output was of such consistently high quality that she is considered one of the great masters of modern American fiction.

She is often associated with what was popularly known as the Southern Renaissance, which included such writers as William Faulkner, Eudora Welty, Truman Capote, Carson McCullers, Katherine Anne Porter, and others. It was a tribute that O'Connor resisted, largely because she felt such a label too often led to the simplistic categorization of her work. "Any fiction that comes out of the South is going to be called grotesque by northern readers—unless it really is grotesque. Then—it is going to be called photographic realism," she once quipped.

O'Connor's talent certainly invites comparison with plenty of writers well above the Mason-Dixon Line. She is often spoken of in the same breath as Ring Lardner or Nathanael West, for the craftsmanship of her humor, characterizations, and dialogue. Her keen awareness of the absurd in daily life is reminiscent of the black comedies of Samuel Beckett and Eugene Ionesco, or the deeply philosophical works of Albert Camus. Her use of the grotesque (another element of the absurd tradition) is perhaps more midwestern than southern, inspired by the father of the American grotesque, Sherwood Anderson.

Yet this is not to say that O'Connor was not a regionalist, for, by her own admission, she undoubtedly was. Her settings, characters, and idioms were all southern; she was proud of the fact that she was part of a longstanding southern tradition of storytelling and clearly shared with Faulkner and Mark Twain the unique southern tendency to wed the comic to the tragic. Perhaps most importantly—and this is what truly ranks her with such modern greats as Faulkner—she had the ability to make the regional become universal, thereby allowing the reader to gain an understanding of the macrocosmic via a narrow, microcosmic slice of life.

Ever since the mid-fifties, when O'Connor's writing began attracting serious critical attention, various charges have been leveled at her by academics and the general reader alike. They have found her stories too depressing, too violent, too obscure and unpredictable. Her biased world vision is too narrow, her landscapes too bleak.

It is true that the world of Flannery O'Connor's fiction can be unsettling. Her settings and characters often appear recognizable enough at first, but there is always that crucial moment in the story when the "scaffolds of reality," as scholar Dorothy Walters so aptly put it, suddenly collapse and "all prior assumptions are challenged and threatened with annihilation."

Yet O'Connor believed that without such violent upheaval there can be no redemption. "[A]scension," as Walters observed, "can only occur as the extension of an initially downward path." If her stories are difficult to read or make us uncomfortable it is because O'Connor believed that personal change is difficult and uncomfortable; so too is the path to redemption in which she placed such unshakable faith. Her intention is always, as Walters notes, "to correct the view of a permissive society which confounds freedom with license and confuses a lax approval with responsible understanding."

Whether or not one agrees with O'Connor's personal vision or theology, they are hard to ignore in the context of her fiction, though some have tried. What remains all but indisputable, however, is the pure beauty of her work, the result of years of dedication and devotion to what she quite genuinely and unegotistically considered a God-given talent.

"I sit there before my typewriter for three hours every day," she once said modestly, "and if anything comes I am there waiting to receive it."

Chronology

March 25, 1925	born in Savannah, Georgia
1931–38	attends parochial school, shows aptitude for writing and drawing; summers spent at mother's family home in Milledgeville
1938	moves with mother to Milledgeville while father takes job in Atlanta and visits on weekends; produces cartoons and articles for high school paper
1940	father forced to retire due to illness, lupus erythematosus, an incurable disease; father dies in February of the following year
1942	graduates from high school and enrolls at Georgia State College for Women (now Georgia College) as a dual sociology and English major; regular contributor to campus publications; sends cartoons to *The New Yorker* but they are rejected
1945–47	attends University of Iowa's Writer's Workshop; "The Geranium," first published story, appears in *Accent* (1946); wins a $750 Rinehart-Iowa Fiction Award and a publishing option by Rinehart for the first four chapters of novel in progress
1948–49	at Yaddo artist's colony in Saratoga Springs, New York; meets other influential writers, editors; leaves Yaddo in '49 and moves to Connecti-

cut to live with Robert and Sally Fitzgerald; hospitalized over Christmas; is later diagnosed with disseminated lupus erythematosus, disease that killed father; begins massive injections of a new experimental cortisone derivative, ACTH

1951 moves with mother to Andalusia, a 1,500-acre farm four miles outside of Milledgeville; can't climb stairs due to hip-weakening ACTH treatment and is confined to first floor; works on revising novel and tends to favorite birds, peacocks

1952 *Wise Blood,* first novel

1955 *A Good Man Is Hard to Find,* short story collection; hip continues to deteriorate, must use crutches to walk

1958 makes pilgrimage to Lourdes and has audience with Pope in Rome; hip temporarily improves; doctors explore possibility of hip operation, but it is deemed too risky

1960 *The Violent Bear It Away*

1964 doctor diagnoses tumor and operates in spite of risk; tumor is removed but lupus is reactivated; spends spring in and out of the hospital; works on stories in hospital bed

August 3, 1964 dies of kidney failure

1965 *Everything That Rises Must Converge* published posthumously

Further Reading

O'Connor's Works

Sally Fitzgerald, editor, *Flannery O'Connor: Collected Works* (New York: Library of America, 1988). Excellent resource containing all the published works (novels and short stories) plus several previously uncollected works in addition to various lectures, essays, and letters. Detailed chronology. Detailed notes on the texts.

Sally Fitzgerald, editor, *Letters of Flannery O'Connor: The Habit of Being* (New York: Farrar, Straus, Giroux, 1979). Extensive selection of O'Connor's letters, offering countless insights into her philosophies and views of fiction; provides initimate portrait. Biographical notes accompany text of letters.

Books About O'Connor

Preston M. Browning, Jr., *Flannery O'Connor* (Carbondale and Edwardsville: Southern Illinois University Press, 1974). Concise but thorough study of the major works. Includes selected bibliography.

Sister Kathleen Feeley, S.S.N.D., *Flannery O'Connor: The Voice of the Peacock* (New Brunswick, New Jersey: Rutgers University Press, 1972). Thorough study of the major works.

Dorothy Tuck MacFarland, *Flannery O'Connor* (New York: Frederick Ungar Publishing Co., 1976). Detailed, but readable study of the novels and short stories. Includes chronology and bibliography.

John Updike
(1932–   )

One of the most gifted and prolific writers in the history of American letters, Harvard-educated John Updike built his reputation on his elegant prose style and insightful portraiture of personal strife among wealthy, middle-class, suburban families.
(National Archives)

*I*n the climactic scene of John Updike's most popular and widely anthologized short story, "A&P," the adolescent hero, Sammy, dramatically quits his job as a grocery store cashier right in the middle of his shift. His is a rather disproportionate act of protest, a chivalrous attempt to salvage the honor of three bathing-suited young beauties (it is summertime) who moments before had been humiliatingly reprimanded by the manager for being indecently dressed in the store. Ignoring the manager's earnest attempt to prevent him from making a mistake he'll regret, Sammy drops his bow tie and apron on the counter and marches off in search of the girls, "but they're gone, of course." The only damsel in distress he finds in the sun-baked asphalt parking lot is a housewife screaming at her children as she packs them into a station wagon. With a sinking feeling in his stomach, Sammy sullenly reflects on "how hard the world was going to be to [him] hereafter."

This gesture on Sammy's part has been called "heroic," a "reflex of the still uncorrupted youth" who has not yet "learned the sad wisdom of compromise," according to Updike scholar Robert Detweiler. A feature of almost every coming-of-age story, this particular lesson is hardly a new one. Yet Sammy's self-determined early retirement from innocence bears greater significance. In Updike's fictive world—where the waters typically run deeper than those of the parable—we discover that "the heroic gesture is often meaningless," as scholar Suzanne Henning Uphaus observes, "and usually arises from selfish rather than unselfish impulses." Sammy quits his job hoping that the girls will notice, but his plan backfires. Thus, his moment of triumph is at the same time one of defeat—just one of the many "embarrassments of middle-class individuals" usually brief "but always painful," as scholar Donald J. Greiner puts it, that so often trigger the conflict in Updike's fiction.

John Updike was under thirty years old when this fairly mature and accomplished story was first published in the pages of *The New Yorker*. By then he had already come and gone as a staff member of the prestigious magazine, where his work has appeared almost exclusively throughout his career; by his 30th birthday, he was the author of two well-received novels, a book of poems, and two short story collections, the then-most recent of which, *Pigeon Feathers and Other Stories* (1962), included "A&P." Today, Updike's impressive tally stands at sixteen novels, ten short story collections, a half-dozen books of poetry, five massive volumes of essays and criticism, one play, and a memoir. And while he recently penned a eulogy for his famed character, Harry "Rabbit"

Angstrom in *Rabbit at Rest* (1990), the final volume of the Rabbit series, Updike, only in his early sixties, shows no signs of slowing down.

The word "prodigy" often arises in most discussions of the life and works of John Updike, one of the most prolific men of letters in the history of American literature. While he is generally recognized as the country's foremost literary commentator on middle- and upper-middle class eastern, suburban WASP culture (rivaled only, perhaps, by the late John Cheever), Updike himself—his own blue blood notwithstanding—actually hails from a fairly humble, working-class background.

The Updikes were originally farmers, dating back to the enterprising Louris Jansen Opdyck who came to New Amsterdam (New York) from Holland in the 17th century, settling in what would later become New Jersey.* By the early 20th century, the family hadn't drifted very far from Trenton until Wesley R. Updike headed west to Pennsylvania in search of work and found a wife, Linda Grace Hoyer. The newlyweds moved in with the bride's parents in a large white house in Shillington, a poor, Pennsylvania Dutch agricultural/mining community where Wesley made a modest living teaching mathematics in the local high school. Their one and only child, John Hoyer Updike, was born on March 18, 1932.

"My boyhood was spent in a world made tranquil by two visible catastrophes: the Depression and World War II," Updike wrote in his 1962 essay "The Dogwood Tree: A Boyhood."† "I was a small-town child," he goes on to report, and Shillington

---

*Another, more distinguished branch of the Updike family acquired land on Narragansett Bay in Rhode Island in 1666 and were among the original settlers of the town of Wickford, once so populated with members of the clan that it was called "Updike Town." Understandably enough, Updike has always nurtured a fondness for this quaint, seaside community, which became the setting (renamed Eastwick) for his 1984 best-seller, *The Witches of Eastwick*. "I am, it could be said, a New Jersey Updike who aspired to be a Rhode Island Updike," wrote the author in his memoirs, *Self-Consciousness* (1989).

† First published in *Five Boyhoods*, edited by Martin Levin (Garden City, New York: Doubleday & Company, Inc., 1962) and later reprinted in *Assorted Prose* (New York: Alfred A Knopf, 1965).

was a typical American small town, with "chicken houses, barns out of plumb, a gunshop, a small lumber mill, a shack where a blind man lived, and the enchanted grotto of a garage whose cement floors had been waxed to the luster of ebony by oil drippings . . ."

Updike distinguished himself in school for his essay-writing skills and otherwise "inched upward from grade to grade," as he recalled in his memoirs, *Self-Consciousness* (1989). Like most children, he "looked forward to Christmas and then to summer." As an adolescent, he read mysteries and P. G. Wodehouse novels borrowed from the public library on trips to the nearby city of Reading. He grew into himself, as he put it, "in the comfortable confines of the local institutions, ethnic tilt, and accent."

Updike would recall the comforts as well as the struggles of these early years in his first novel, *The Poorhouse Fair* (1959) and in the short fiction collection, *Olinger Stories* (1964). *Poorhouse*'s sad plot (set in the then-future year of 1977) about a man who dies of discouragement after he and his sister fail to make a go of a country store/gas station is a story "not of heroic men but of little people living little lives," according to Greiner in his study of Updike's novels. *The Poorhouse Fair,* Greiner goes on to suggest, established the starting point of a continuous thread running through many of Updike's works which concerns "either nostalgia for the small-town, rural past or delineation of the small-town, urban present."

Shillington provided the model for the small town of Olinger (pronounced "Oh-linger") in *Olinger Stories,* as well as in *Pigeon Feathers and Other Stories* and *The Music School* (1966). In all three short story collections, Updike continued to explore "the primary tensions between rural and urban values," as scholar Larry E. Taylor observed in his study of the pastoral tradition in Updike's fiction. Updike developed this theme more fully in *The Centaur* (1963).

Rich as they were in material for a young writer, these post-Depression years were hard on Updike's family, relying as they all did—Linda's parents included—on Wesley's meager teaching salary. When that disappeared during the summers, the senior Updike took odd jobs while Linda sold asparagus and pansies from her garden, an enterprise which embarrassed her increasingly self-conscious young son. In 1945, hard times finally forced the family to sell the big white house in town and move to nearby Plowville. There they lived in relative isolation on the farm where Linda had been born.

While Updike disliked the solitude, he took the opportunity to concentrate on writing in addition to drawing, which was his first love. He hoped one day to be a cartoonist and publish his drawings in *Collier's, The New Yorker,* or any of the other publications that "called out" to him "with the slick voice of New York" from the magazine rack at Ibach's soda fountain. It was Linda Updike, an aspiring author herself, who encouraged and inspired her son to pursue a literary career. She was determined that young John should go to Harvard because the prestigious university had produced so many fine writers. Updike won a full scholarship and in the fall of 1950 arrived in Cambridge, Massachusetts—a wide-eyed, mud-stained country lad standing before the ivy-covered gates of one of the foremost centers of learning in the world.

"I had a lot to learn when I came to Harvard, which was fortunate, since Harvard had a lot to teach," Updike recalled in a short piece written for *The Harvard Gazette* on the occasion of his thirtieth reunion.* For a student of Updike's ready intellect, Harvard was an invaluable resource, providing both polish and the foundation for his erudite, sophisticated, and highly artistic prose style. "I read what they told me and was much the better for it," Updike states in his memoirs.

It was a heady, romantic era in which to be an English major, especially at Harvard, which attracted the likes of T. S. Eliot, Robert Frost, Dylan Thomas, Thornton Wilder, and Vladimir Nabokov as lecturers or visiting faculty. "Literature was in. Pop music was Patti Page and Perry Como, the movies were Doris Day and John Wayne, and youth culture was something that

---

* Later included in the nonfiction collection *Odd Jobs* (1991).

happened, if anywhere, at summer camp," Updike reflected in his piece for the *Gazette.*

Cambridge being the cradle of liberalism, however, there were demonstrations, albeit orderly ones, staged by politically passionate Harvard students. While Updike totted placards alongside his "Unitarian, tennis-sneakered, pony-tailed girl-friend" outside the polling booths, this Lutheran Democrat from the farmlands of Pennsylvania was always conscious of the social gulf that existed between him and his classmates. "They, secure in the upper-middle class, were Democrats out of human sympathy and humanitarian largesse, because this was the party that helped the poor. Our family had simply *been* poor, and voted Democrat out of crude self-interest," he confessed in his memoirs.

One place Updike did feel at home was at the offices of the *Harvard Lampoon,* the college's venerable and famed humor publication. A nervous freshman clutching a handful of cartoons and sketches, Updike walked through the doors of the *Lampoon*'s colorful brick building—with its "rank deep smell of old magazines subaqueously stored in the basement"—and eventually became the editor, contributing numerous cartoons, poems, and essays throughout his four years at college. Although he claimed to have never understood the "social engineering" that drove the infamous publication, Updike concluded that he "was delighted to be asked along," as he put it in a tributary essay in honor of the *Lampoon*'s hundredth anniversary.

During his sophomore year, Updike met and fell in love with Mary Pennington, a Radcliffe fine-arts major and the daughter of a Unitarian minister. They married the following year and upon Updike's graduation in 1954 the couple moved to Oxford, England where Updike studied at the Ruskin School of Drawing and Fine Art on a year-long fellowship. While in England, the Updikes' first child, Elizabeth was born. Also in 1954, Updike was thrilled to publish his first story, "Friends from Philadelphia," in the pages of *The New Yorker.*

While in England, Updike was visited by *New Yorker* editor E. B. White, who offered the bright young author a position as

The classic New England coastal town of Ipswich, Massachusetts, where Updike lived and worked for twenty years, provided inspiration for many of his stories and novels.
(Tom Verde)

a staff writer. The job was a long-awaited dream come true for Updike—an entree into "a club of sorts, from within which the large rest of literary America . . . could be politely disdained." The Updikes returned to America and moved into an apartment on Riverside Drive in New York City. From 1955 to 1957, Updike produced witty, urbane prose sketches for the "Talk of the Town" column, in addition to contributing various poems, stories, and essays.

After two years of immersion in New York's suffocating literary "scene," Updike decided that he had had enough. He felt the best way for him to pursue his artistic career was to escape the scene altogether. With a new baby, David, and the rest of the family in tow, Updike moved to the idyllic North Shore town of Ipswich, Massachusetts, where he bought an old fixer-upper of a house and dove headlong into suburban New England middle-class life. He worked at home in a small second-floor room until, with the advent of two more children, Michael and Miranda, the house became too chaotic and he rented an office above a restaurant in town. He also became actively involved in town meetings and local politics, the Congregational church, the golf club, and an amateur musical group.

His first book, *The Carpentered Hen* (1958), a collection of poems, was largely ignored but his novel *The Poorhouse Fair* and the short story collection *The Same Door* (1959) received wide praise. In 1960 he published perhaps his most famous and some say his most powerful novel, *Rabbit, Run*, a disturbing book that shocked readers with its explicit sex scenes and grim situations.

The novel's troubled protagonist is Harry "Rabbit" Angstrom, a twenty-six-year-old former high-school basketball star who finds adult life a disappointment after the glory days of his adolescence. He feels trapped and oppressed by maturity's relentless demands: family, job, responsibility. When life's events begin to overwhelm him, Harry Angstrom begins his flight.

Why Rabbit is constantly running, of course, is the central question of the novel—a question with a variety of answers. On one level, Rabbit is fleeing the "claustrophobic nature of our institutions," as one critic put it—the troubled economy, television, advertising, the pressures of family life, organized religion, middle-class morality, etc.

Yet Rabbit's running represents pursuit as well as flight, "a search for meaning beyond the natural world," as scholar Suzanne Henning Uphaus put it. "[S]omewhere behind all this," Rabbit says, "there's something that wants me to find it." Society's conventions—marriage, family, work, church—all fail to bring Rabbit any closer to what "it" is. Paradoxically, he seeks the spiritual via the physical, namely sports and sex, which in his mind are often indistinguishable.

But in the end, for Updike, "the body can never satisfy the needs of the spirit," as Uphaus put it, and sex is ultimately a nontranscendental experience. This is the lesson that Rabbit fails to learn and that keeps him constantly running in the wrong direction in a state of angst-ridden (hence his name) moral confusion. By grafting religious meaning onto earthly experiences—basketball, golf, sex—Rabbit has trapped himself, instead of being trapped by others, "in a contemporary physical world that prevents spiritual faith," as Uphaus observes.

The publication of *Rabbit, Run* focused considerable attention on its twenty-seven-year-old author, primarily because of its graphic treatment of sexuality in the context of a work of serious literature. "If the power to shock may be taken as a yardstick of fiction," *Time* magazine announced, "John Updike has written one of the year's most important novels." The critics generally agreed that Updike was a brilliant stylist, but were troubled by the grittiness of his plots. He continued to attract mixed reviews with his next few books, *Pigeon Feathers and Other Stories, The Centaur,* and *Of the Farm* (1965).

The Centaur is a retelling of the classical Greek myth of Chiron—the noblest of the Centaurs who gives up his immortality to help Prometheus—set in Olinger with a science teacher in the role of Chiron and his fifteen-year-old son as Prometheus. Updike had originally conceived the novel as a companion piece to *Rabbit, Run*—two different approaches to "the game of life," as he recalled in a 1990 *New York Times Book Review* testimonial to his character: "[O]ne would be the rabbit approach, a kind of dodgy approach—spontaneous, unreflective, frightened . . . and the second was to be the horse method of coping with life, to get into the harness and pull your load until you drop. And this was eventually *The Centaur.*"

Though it perplexed some reviewers, *The Centaur* won Updike the prestigious National Book Award and led to his election to the National Institute of Arts and Letters—at thirty-two, the youngest man ever to be so honored. What had been a risky experiment, i.e., leaving the security of his job at *The*

John Updike

New Yorker and the high visibility of life in the New York literary fast lane, had paid off for Updike.

"By my mid-thirties, through diligence and daring, I had arrived at a lifestyle we might call genteel bohemian," he recalled in his memoirs. "[N]ice old house . . . four dusty but healthy children with Sunday bests at the backs of their closets, two cars, one of them a convertible, and, for dinner, lots of rice casseroles and California wine. To me, this was prosperity."

He had escaped "the muddy farm in Pennsylvania with its outhouse and coal-oil stove," and gained entry to a privileged world of private schools, cocktail parties, and country clubs. Yet while the upper-class environment has, by and large, been his milieu, he confessed in his memoirs that it was never of any real interest to him:

> I saw myself as a literary spy within average, public-school, super-market America. It was there I felt comfortable; it was there that I felt the real news was. I wrote short stories for The New Yorker all those years like an explorer sending bulletins from the bush, and they published most of them, and my prosperity slowly drove me upwards in the social scale to a stratum that I thought was already well enough covered, by Marquand, Cheever, and others.

Updike's modesty about sharing a stage with the likes of Marquand[*] and Cheever notwithstanding, he is generally considered one of modern literature's keenest observers of American middle- and upper-middle class marital life. Again and again, he has returned to this environment in order to mine material for what has been one of his central themes: the inherent conflicts, rooted deeply in the faith of his Protestant ancestors, that arise from the dual nature of human beings as creatures of both carnal desires and spiritual longings.

---

[*]J[ohn]. P [hillips]. Marquand (1893–1960)—American novelist best known for his witty, amusing, and sympathetic treatments of aristocratic New England families (especially the Boston "Brahmin" class) striving to maintain their antiquated, Puritan standards in the face of an increasingly egalitarian, twentieth-century American society. Among Marquand's best-known such studies is The Late George Apley.

Because faith is so difficult to maintain in a "contemporary world indifferent to spiritual values," as Uphaus put it—where church and state are Constitutionally divided and all modesty has been trampled by the permissiveness of the sexual revolution—Updike's protagonists often heed the call of their sensual desires at the expense of their spiritual progress. His novels and short stories are rife with lustful ministers and minister's wives, unfaithful husbands, drunken, wife-swapping cocktail parties, boozy car accidents, and compromised faith. Yet all this takes place in an environment where keeping up appearances is crucial, where the veneer of morality must be carefully maintained, like a front lawn, else the delicately balanced social system will collapse upon itself.

"My characters are very fond of both safety and freedom, and yet the two things don't go together quite," Updike told *U.S. News & World Report* in a 1986 interview, "so they're in a state of tension all the time."

Making the ethical, safe decision (monogamy, marriage, family responsibility) is often difficult for Updike's characters. In other words, it's usually much easier (and more fun) to be bad than good. Updike's characters recognize this, and often take the easier path, despite the consequences.

Updike explores this dilemma throughout many of his novels—most notably *Couples* (1968), *A Month of Sundays* (1975), and *Marry Me* (1976)—and in the dozens of short stories he produced for *The New Yorker* and other publications during the sixties and seventies, many of which are collected in *The Music School* and *Museums & Women and Other Stories* (1972).

A tour which Updike made in 1964–65 to Russia and several eastern European countries as part of the U.S.S.R.–U.S. Cultural Exchange Program provided partial inspiration for the character of Henry Bech, a Jewish American writer who made his first appearance in the O. Henry Award–winning story "The Bulgarian Poetess."[*] "[N]ever wanting to let a good thing go unflogged," as Updike put it, he produced a half dozen more witty

---

[*] First published in *The New Yorker* and later reprinted in *The Music School*.

stories of Bech's struggle with writer's block and the world around him in *Bech: A Book* (1970).

Having abandoned an attempt at a historical novel about the life of James Buchanan, Pennsylvania's only President,[*] Updike revived his character Harry Angstrom in *Rabbit Redux* (1971). Rabbit and his wife are back together, but break up once more in this examination of marital strife, set against the backdrop of one of the most turbulent eras in the nation's history.

"[T]here was all this distress around me," Updike recalled in his *New York Times Book Review* essay, "Why Rabbit Had to Go." "Vietnam distress, race riots, marches, agitation of all sorts. Suddenly it seemed to me that Rabbit Angstrom of Pennsylvania, about whose future some people had expressed curiosity, might be the vehicle in which to package some of the American unease that was raging all around us."

War, drugs, racial tensions, the space age, the sexual revolution—all of these highly charged topics unfold in the pages of this well-received sequel. Rabbit, Updike's enduring everyman, stands by his country as it comes under siege in changing times, much as Updike himself did during these troubled years, the violence of which he claims "amazed and alarmed" him.

In the mid-seventies, Updike refocused his attention inward, from national issues to the private politics of marriage, especially his own, which by 1974 had disintegrated to the breaking point.

"My children sensed the crisis," he recalled in *Self-Consciousness*. "I painfully glimpsed my younger son, fifteen years old in those last months when I lived with him, angrily throwing [the cat] down the cellar stairs; the boy had tears of exasperation in his eyes. In the end, rather than discomfit the cats, I discomfited the human beings of my family and moved to Boston."

Updike fictionalized such painful scenes and others from the years leading up to his eventual divorce in 1976 in numerous

---

[*]Updike later recycled the fruits of his research into Buchanan's life in his only play to date, *Buchanan Dying* (1974). Buchanan also figures prominently in Updike's 1992 novel *Memories of the Ford Administration.*

short stories, many of which can be found in *Museums &
Women, Problems and Other Stories*, and *Too Far to Go* (1979).

"The Taste of Metal," "Your Lover Just Called," "Eros Ram-
pant," and "The Orphaned Swimming Pool" are fine examples
of Updike's eloquent yet emotionally taut examinations of the
anguish of infidelity. Stories such as "Daughter, Last Glimpses
of," "Nevada," "Domestic Life in America," and "Separating"
provide poignant and moving still lifes of families in the midst
of divorce. One almost recognizes in the final paragraphs of
"Separating" the painful true-life scene Updike described
about his own son:

> *Richard bent to kiss an averted face but his son, sinewy, turned
> and with wet cheeks embraced him and gave him a kiss . . . In his
> father's ear he moaned one word, the crucial, intelligent word:
> "Why?"*
> Why. *It was a whistle of wind in a crack, a knife thrust, a
> window thrown open on emptiness. The white face was gone, the
> darkness was featureless. Richard had forgotten why.*

Some of the stories in *Too Far to Go* appeared earlier in other
collections. Called "the Maples stories," they concern "the
decline and fall" of the marriage of New Englanders, Richard
and Joan Maple, and were adapted in 1979 as a critically
acclaimed television production. Unpleasant as the subject
matter may seem, Updike, in his foreword to *Too Far to Go*,
points out that these tales also focus on many happy times as
well, "of growing children and a million mundane moments
shared." The moral of the Maples stories, he concludes, is "that
all blessings are mixed."

After living in Boston for two years, Updike moved back to
the North Shore, to the village of Georgetown, and a year later
married Martha Bernhard, a woman seven years his junior and
the ex-wife of a Boston law executive. The couple later moved
to Beverly, Massachusetts, another North Shore town. In 1982,
an older, though seemingly no wiser, Bech returns in *Bech Is
Back*. Updike gathered material for Bech's world tour ("Bech

Third-Worlds It") during his own tour of Africa as a Fulbright lecturer in 1973. The trip also inspired *The Coup* (1978), about the militaristic takeover and Marxist rule of a fictitious African nation. The novel is considered among Updike's most complex and one of the few not set in the WASPy Northeast.

Though time is catching up with him, Rabbit is back once more in *Rabbit Is Rich* (1981), this time as a grandfather, though still as sexually confused as ever and running on empty as the book's opening passage, "Running out of gas . . ." implies. Rabbit is a wealthy car dealer now, making a fortune selling Toyotas during the gas shortage of the Carter administration, but his life is unfulfilled. His son, Nelson, is now a college-aged ingrate—"[c]ynical, lazy and tantrum-prone . . . Updike's case study in the perils of permissive parenting," as *GQ*'s Walter Kirn put it in his retrospective on the Rabbit series.

Updike was awarded a Pulitzer Prize for *Rabbit Is Rich,* as well as an American Book Award and the Edward MacDowell Medal for literature. Regarded as one of Updike's lightest novels, *Rabbit Is Rich* represents yet another set of self-taught lessons for Harry Angstrom, as Updike observes: "[T]o be rich is just another way of being poor, that your needs expand with your income and the world eventually takes away what it gives."

The balance of power, in keeping with the social revolution of the times, shifts in Updike's next novel, *The Witches of Eastwick,* in which a trio of friends (Alexandra, Sukie, and Jane) in a small New England town divorce their husbands and take back control of their lives. They do so (Updike leads us to believe) by hexing their former spouses into a jar of dust, a sprig of dried herbs, and a placemat, respectively. The mysterious stranger who comes to town, Darryl Van Horne, (the devil, again as Updike indicates) tries to manipulate and divide the women, but in doing so teaches them how to acquire more power. "So this is what men had been murmuring about, monopolizing all these centuries, death;" muses Jane, as she reflects on a dispatched enemy, "no wonder they had kept it to themselves, no wonder they had kept it from women . . ."

The discovery of scientific proof of the existence of God stimulates the action in Updike's next novel, *Roger's Version* (1986) while in the short story collection, *Trust Me* (1987) the author pries back the lid of suburban, domestic life once more to reveal its benefits and blemishes. "Man was not meant to abide in paradise," is the conclusion of the narrator of the story "The Ideal Village"; the instability of domestic life, as stressed in these stories, appears to confirm this gloomy assumption. American womanhood, romance, and the lighter side of religion are the topics Updike addressed in his next book, *S.*, in which Sarah Worth, a latter-day Hester Prynne, heads west in search of love and spiritual renewal.

The final volume of the Rabbit series, *Rabbit at Rest*, appeared almost a decade after what many had thought had already been Harry Angstrom's last adventure. Fifty-five years old and in semiretirement, Rabbit spends his winters in Florida where his cocaine-snorting son Nelson comes for a visit with his wife Pru and their two children. Rabbit suffers a heart attack and the long novel (the longest of the series) keeps pace with the dying man's faltering heart.

Updike ends his character's thirty-year saga just as he began it, with Rabbit, the athletic has-been, begging some kid to let him shoot a few baskets, trying to prove to youth that he himself was once young. "The hoop fills his circle of vision, it descends to kiss hip lips, he can't miss." One final glorious jump shot for Rabbit, and it is over—his heart "bursts" and he is just "a big old white man" lying in the dust in his Bermuda shorts and golf shirt.

"[A] depressed book, about a depressed man, written by a depressed man," Updike concluded in his essay, "Why Rabbit Had to Go." Many critics have agreed that it is just as well that Updike has laid his most famous character to rest. In an age of AIDS and the fall of communism, there is no room left in the world for the promiscuous and opinionated Harry Angstrom, a product of the Cold War and of Cold War attitudes and values.

In 1992, Updike finally got the chance to publicize his love affair with "Pennsylvania's only, much-maligned president,"

John Updike

James Buchanan, in *Memories of the Ford Administration.* Placing the responsibility of telling Buchanan's story in the hands of fictional historian Alf Clayton, who has been commissioned to produce a memoir of the Ford administration as well, Updike created a surreal nineteenth/twentieth century "New England sex comedy," as he told *Vogue*, unrestrained by a pure historical novel's demands for accuracy.

Updike felt equally unshackled when composing his most recent novel, *Brazil* (1994), set in the lush jungles and steamy cities of that South American country, where love and sorcery blend in a Latinized retelling of the Tristan and Iseult legend.[*] When asked by *The New York Times Book Review* what he knew of Brazilian sorcery, shamans, and landscapes, Updike replied "I made it up," although in truth the book's afterword reveals numerous sources upon which he relied for inspiration and details.

In his memoir, Updike likened his artistic journey to "a kind of bicycle," which, "if I were ever to stop pedaling, would dump me flat on my side." Along that journey, some critics have called him an elegant stylist who nonetheless lacks depth, who has simply never had very much to say. Then again, there are those who find him deeply insightful, but have longed for him to cut the verbiage and get out of his own way. Whatever the final verdict, it is clear that few writers in the history of American letters have pedaled quite so fast or so far as John Updike.

---

[*] Medieval story cycle of Celtic origin; forbidden love is at the center of the Tristan and Iseult legend, considered one of the world's greatest love stories.

Chronology

March 18, 1932	born in Shillington, Pennsylvania
1945	family moves to farm in Plowville
1950	enrolls at Harvard University on full scholarship; serves as editor of *Harvard Lampoon*
1953	marries Radcliffe student Mary Pennington
1954	graduates Harvard and moves to Oxford, England on year-long scholarship to Ruskin School of Drawing and Fine Art; first child, Elizabeth born; first story, "Friends from Philadelphia," published in *The New Yorker;* accepts job offer from *New Yorker* editor E. B. White
1955–57	at *New Yorker;* writes "Talk of the Town" and other pieces
1957	quits *New Yorker* and moves to Ipswich, Massachusetts; continues to write short stories for *New Yorker* and becomes actively involved in local community affairs
1959	*Poorhouse Fair,* first novel; *The Same Door,* collection of short stories
1960	*Rabbit, Run*
1963	*The Centaur*
1964–65	to Russia and Eastern Europe as part of cultural exchange program
1968	*Couples*

John Updike

1971   *Rabbit Redux*

1974–77   separates from wife; moves to apartment in Boston; divorces in 1976, moves to Georgetown, Massachusetts and a year later marries Martha Bernhard

1979   *Problems and Other Stories* and *Too Far to Go;* both collections contain numerous stories focusing on marriage and divorce

1981   *Rabbit Is Rich;* novel wins Pulitzer Prize

1984   *The Witches of Eastwick*

1990   *Rabbit at Rest*

1994   *Brazil*

1995   *Orchid Adele Crockett Robertson*

Further Reading

Works by Updike

Rabbit, Run (New York: Alfred A. Knopf, 1960). The first book in Updike's Rabbit series which introduces his "everyman" character, Harry "Rabbit" Angstrom.

Pigeon Feathers and Other Stories (New York: Alfred A. Knopf, 1962). Updike's second collection of short stories. Includes his most famous story, "A&P."

The Centaur (New York: Alfred A. Knopf, 1963). A retelling of the myth of Chiron, set in Updike's fictional town of Olinger, Pennsylvania.

The Music School (New York: Alfred A. Knopf, 1966). Tales inspired by Updike's younger years in Shillington and in Ipswich.

Couples (New York: Alfred A. Knopf, 1968). Infidelity and marital tension in middle-class America.

Rabbit Redux (New York: Alfred A. Knopf, 1971). Rabbit is ten years older and facing the challenges of a changing society in this sequel to Updike's most famous novel.

A Month of Sundays (New York: Alfred A. Knopf, 1975). A minister's lusty misadventures with the women of his parish.

Too Far to Go: The Maples Stories (New York: Fawcett Crest, 1979). Updike's saga of a marriage in decline.

Rabbit Is Rich (New York: Alfred A. Knopf, 1981). Despite his properity, Rabbit remains destitute in his soul.

Hugging the Shore (New York: Alfred A. Knopf, 1983). Third collection of the author's essays and criticism. Casts greater light on Updike's literary life and times.

Self-Consciousness (New York: Alfred A. Knopf, 1989). An author's look back at the history of his career.

Rabbit at Rest (New York: Alfred A. Knopf, 1990). Updike's elegant swan song for Harry Angstrom.

Odd Jobs (New York: Alfred A. Knopf, 1991). More essays and criticisms; includes Updike's own thoughts on many of his works.

Books About Updike

Robert Detweiler, *John Updike* (Boston: Twayne Publishers, 1984). Comprehensive study of the major works and selected stories up to and including *Bech Is Back*. Brief biographical essay, chronology, bibliography.

Donald J. Greiner, *John Updike's Novels* (Athens, Ohio: Ohio University Press, 1984). Detailed study of the novels in the context of Updike's life, up to and including *Rabbit Is Rich*.

David Thorburn and Howard Eiland, editors, *John Updike: A Collection of Critical Essays* (Englewood Cliffs, N.J.: Prentice-Hall, Inc. 1979). Collection of critical essays by many of the major Updike scholars.

Suzanna Henning Uphaus, *John Updike* (New York: Frederick Ungar Publishing Co., 1980). Comprehensive and insightful study of selected short stories and the major works up to and including *The Coup*. Excellent introduction which examines Updike's major themes.

Index

Bold numbers indicate main headings; *italic* numbers indicate illustrations and captions; italic numbers followed by *"t"* indicate chronology; *"n"* indicates footnote.

Index

Index